WTO: THE DOHA AGENDA
The New Negotiations on World Trade

Bhagirath Lal Das

Zed Books Ltd.
London and New York

TWN
Third World Network
Penang, Malaysia

WTO: THE DOHA AGENDA
THE NEW NEGOTIATIONS ON WORLD TRADE
is published by
Third World Network
121-S, Jalan Utama
10450 Penang, Malaysia.
Email: twnet@po.jaring.my
Website: www.twnside.org

and

Zed Books Ltd.
7 Cynthia Street
London, N1 9JF, UK
and Room 400, 175 Fifth Avenue
New York, NY 10010, USA.

Distributed exclusively in the United States
on behalf of Zed Books by Palgrave,
a division of St Martin's Press, LLC
175 Fifth Avenue
New York, NY 10010, USA.

Printed by Jutaprint
2 Solok Sungei Pinang 3, Sg. Pinang
11600 Penang, Malaysia.

ISBN   1 84277 298 8hb (Zed)
ISBN   1 84277 299 6pb (Zed)
ISBN   983 9747 84 3 (TWN)

US CIP data ia available from the Library of Congress.
British Cataloguing-in-Publication Data is available from the British Library.

CONTENTS

PART II: SOME SUGGESTIONS FOR IMPROVEMENT IN THE WTO AGREEMENTS

PREFACE

THIS book by Bhagirath Lal Das provides an analysis of the new agenda of negotiations and discussions in the World Trade Organisation arising from the important WTO Ministerial Conference in Doha, Qatar, in November 2001.

The Doha meeting resulted in a lengthy agenda with many issues meant to be discussed in a short period (to be concluded in January 2005). As Das points out, this represents a much heavier programme than that of the Uruguay Round (the comprehensive set of negotiations that ended with the establishment of the WTO). It involves an extremely heavy workload especially for delegations from developing countries which are usually small and lacking in human resources and in financial and technical capacity.

More importantly, the issues mandated for negotiations and discussions are of immense significance for the development prospects of the developing countries that are Members of the WTO. Many policy makers in these countries, as well as analysts and academics, have already voiced serious concerns on how the existing WTO rules have narrowed the scope and options that developing countries have in pursuit of their socio-economic and development goals. The Doha programme has the potential to increase these problems.

This timely book by Das, who is widely acknowledged as an international authority on trade issues and multilateral trade rules, throws light on the major issues that are currently under negotiation and discussion under the Doha programme. It also provides conceptual and concrete proposals on how developing-country Members of the WTO should respond to the programme. We are glad to publish this important guide to the latest

WTO negotiations and discussions which will have such a significant influence on the future shape of the globalisation process.

The book is in two Parts. Part I provides an overview of the Doha work programme, and analyses 14 of its key issues, including the topics currently under intense negotiations (agriculture, services, industrial products, intellectual property); the developing countries' proposals to reform or improve the present rules (implementation issues); and the controversial "new issues" (investment, competition policy, transparency in government procurement, trade facilitation) which the developed countries have been trying to push (and which many developing countries have been trying to resist) as subjects for new agreements. For each item, Das provides an analysis of the issue and proposes positions that developing countries could take.

Part II contains in more detailed form a set of suggestions for improving some of the existing WTO agreements and rules. This is a useful complement to Part I as discussions in the earlier part of the book often refer to problems which are then taken up in Part II as concrete proposals and measures that can be put forward to rectify the problems. Part II is based on an earlier paper by Das that has been extensively referred to by policy makers and delegations of developing countries.

The book also reproduces the Ministerial Declaration issued at the WTO's Doha conference, for easy reference by the reader.

This latest book by Das could be usefully read together with two earlier books by the author, *An Introduction to the WTO Agreements* and *The WTO Agreements: Deficiencies, Imbalances and Required Changes*. Both have also been published by the Third World Network and Zed Books.

Martin Khor
Director, Third World Network

Part I

THE NEW WORK PROGRAMME OF THE WTO

1 INTRODUCTION

The new Work Programme of the World Trade Organization (WTO) emerging out of the WTO's Doha Ministerial Conference in November 2001 involves a very heavy workload particularly for the developing countries. It is a much heavier programme than that of the Uruguay Round of multilateral trade negotiations (which resulted in the establishment of the WTO). Almost all the major items of the Uruguay Round, like agriculture, services, subsidies, anti-dumping, regional trading arrangements, dispute settlement, industrial tariffs and some aspects of TRIPS (trade-related aspects of intellectual property rights), form part of the negotiations in the Work Programme. Environment has also been included in the subjects of negotiation. Besides, intense work is envisaged on the "Singapore issues" (i.e., the new areas of investment, competition policy, transparency in government procurement and trade facilitation) as well as in the area of electronic commerce. The short time span of three years set for this work makes the task particularly arduous for the developing countries.

IMBALANCE ENHANCED

The new Work Programme significantly enhances the imbalance in the WTO system. For several years the developing countries have been drawing attention to the severe imbalances and inequities in the WTO agreements. The Work Programme, instead of eliminating the imbalance, has in fact enhanced it by giving special treatment to the areas of interest to the major developed countries and ignoring the areas of interest to the developing countries. Negotiations have been launched in a new area, viz., environment, and the level of work has been enhanced and intensified in the areas of the Singapore issues and electronic commerce. All these have been subjects of deep interest to the major developed countries, while the developing countries have been resisting their being taken up in the WTO. The main proposals of the developing countries were those grouped as "implementation issues", where practically nothing has been done, as will be explained later. The issues of great importance to many of them, e.g., textiles and balance-of-payments provisions, do not feature in the main text of the Work Programme.

Even the inclusion of the subjects of finance and technology is hardly significant for the developing countries as the work envisaged in these fields is of a very general and broad nature. Similar is the situation regarding the clause on special and differential treatment for the developing countries, which aims at making the provisions on such treatment contained in the WTO agreements more precise, effective and operational. There are very few special and differential provisions which reduce the substantive levels of obligations of the developing countries. Hence this clause in the Work Programme is hardly of great benefit to the developing countries.

The Work Programme is a gain for the major developed countries, but they have given nothing in return to the developing countries. This is totally contrary to the expectation in the GATT/WTO process that reciprocity is to be the main guiding principle in negotiations. Reciprocity should not be assessed only in terms of specific commitments in agreements, but also in the selection of items to be accorded special attention in the agenda of the WTO. Sadly, the new phase of the WTO's work has started with an enhancement of the existing imbalance.

Ironically the Work Programme has been sometimes termed a "development agenda", which is quite erroneous. As mentioned above and as will be explained below, the agenda of the Work Programme has been totally set by the major developed countries guided by their own economic interests. The priority of the development of the developing countries is not reflected in it.

CHANGE IN NEGOTIATING PATTERN

Such a one-sided outcome of the Doha Ministerial Conference has been made possible by the changing pattern of the GATT/WTO negotiations. The Work Programme is not the result of any serious negotiation among the membership of the WTO. The major developed countries have not engaged in any negotiation of a give-and-take type; they just put up their proposals and asked the developing countries to accept them. The reports which emanated from the Doha Ministerial Conference about its procedural aspects have indicated that the developing countries were put under various types of pressures, particularly towards the end of the Conference. Ultimately their will withered and they gave in to the demands of the major developed countries. (Of course, there were some face-saving minor adjustments here and there.) This newly emerging pattern of the WTO process is very disturbing. If the developing countries do not guard against it and defend themselves, they will be losing further ground.

The Work Programme is now in position and the major developed countries will certainly try to build on it rapidly. It is therefore desirable for the developing countries to understand the implications of the various elements of the Work Programme, use it to their advantage as much as possible and minimize emerging damage. The following chapters are aimed at assisting them in this process.

2 IMPLEMENTATION ISSUES (PARA. 12)

The implementation issues are addressed in paragraph 12 of the Doha Ministerial Declaration and in the Doha Ministerial Decision on Implementation-Related Issues and Concerns. These two sets of provisions have to be considered together. Before examining the action to be taken, it is relevant to consider the background of this subject.

In the process of preparation for the Seattle Ministerial Conference in 1999, the developing countries had listed out a number of proposals in various areas of the WTO agreements. The proposals have been put together in the WTO General Council document JOB(01)/14 of 20 February 2001 with the title "Implementation-Related Issues and Concerns". There are some additional proposals in the WTO document JOB(01)152/Rev.1 of 27 October 2001 with the title "Compilation of Outstanding Implementation Issues Raised by Members". These two documents should be considered together to enable one to form a comprehensive picture of the list of implementation issues.

These proposals emerged out of the developing countries' experience of the implementation of the WTO agreements in their own countries and also in the developed countries. Some of these proposals involved improvement of the WTO agreements and their operation. The developing countries attached a lot of importance to these proposals and, in fact, during the preparation for the Doha Ministerial Conference they said that these proposals must first be addressed effectively before negotiations were launched in any new area. But the ultimate treatment of these implementation proposals in the Doha Ministerial Declaration and Ministerial Decision has been very disappointing.

The Ministerial Decision on implementation is a long document, but it has very little substance. The only concrete and substantive decisions contained therein are the following:

(i)   The agreements on Sanitary and Phytosanitary Measures and Technical Barriers to Trade provide for "a reasonable interval" between the publication of a measure or a standard and its coming into force. The Decision says that this interval shall not normally be less than six months.

(ii) The Agreement on Sanitary and Phytosanitary Measures provides for "longer time-frames for compliance" with the measures in respect of products of interest to the developing countries. The Decision says that this time-frame shall not normally be less than six months.

(iii) The Agreement on Subsidies and Countervailing Measures has given some concessions regarding subsidies to developing countries which have a per capita Gross National Product (GNP) of less than US$1,000 per year. The Decision says that a developing country will continue to fall under this category until it reaches this level of GNP for three consecutive years. Also, if a country has been excluded from this category as a result of its achieving this level of GNP, the Decision says that it will be re-included when its GNP per capita falls below this level.

The inclusion of "normally" in items (i) and (ii) above has, however, made the stated time limits very much voluntary.

The rest of the Decision contains operative phrases like: "reaffirms", (a particular WTO body) "is directed to give further consideration", "urges

Members", "takes note of", (a particular WTO body) "is instructed to review", "requests" (a WTO body) "to examine", "confirms the approach", "shall examine with special care", "recognizes", "underlines the importance", "agrees that ... interim arrangements ... shall be consistent", "agrees that (a WTO body) shall continue its review", "directs (a WTO body) to extend the transition period", (a WTO body) "is directed to continue its examination", etc.

The irony is that despite such thin content, paragraph 12 of the Ministerial Declaration starts with the high-sounding statement: "We attach the utmost importance to the implementation-related issues ... and are determined to find appropriate solutions to them". And some later reports have commented favourably by referring to the adoption of "around 50 decisions" by the Ministers at Doha "involving hard bargaining". As the explanation given above shows, only three decisions are of a concrete nature, while the rest merely entail continuing consideration of the issues.

Paragraph 12 of the Declaration lays down three tracks of institutional arrangements for continuing the consideration:

(i)   In some of its paragraphs, the Decision has instructed certain WTO bodies to take up/continue the work.

(ii) The issues which are relevant to a "specific negotiating mandate" in the Declaration will be addressed under that mandate. This provision is somewhat unclear. Most likely it means that the issues which fall in any broad area, like agriculture, subsidies, anti-dumping, etc., where negotiation has been mandated will be taken up by the body handling that negotiation. Thus the implementation issues relating to anti-dumping, for example, will be handled by the negotiating body handling "Rules".

(iii) The remaining issues will be handled by the relevant existing Councils, Committees, etc. of the WTO.

In respect of the third track mentioned above, there is a provision that these existing bodies will take up the issues as a matter of priority and report by the end of 2002 to the Trade Negotiations Committee established to oversee the negotiations under the Work Programme. In respect of a few issues in the first track also, some final dates have been prescribed in the Decision.

POINTS OF STRENGTH

The points of strength for the developing countries in the Declaration and the Decision in terms of pursuing the implementation issues are the following:

(i)   The Declaration says that this exercise is "an integral part" of the Work Programme. Hence it cannot be left by the wayside while working on the Work Programme.

(ii) The Ministers say in the Declaration that they "attach the utmost importance" to these issues and "are determined" to find solutions to them. Further, in the preamble to the Decision, the Ministers declare themselves determined "to take concrete action" on these issues raised by the developing countries. In view of such strong political expressions, it is quite rational for the developing countries to expect that this subject should be accorded the highest priority in the Work Programme. Hence, they will be justified in suggesting that these issues should be taken up for consideration and solution as the earliest part of the agenda of the relevant WTO bodies involved in the three tracks mentioned above.

(iii) Specific dates have been mentioned for completion of work on several items. It is thus expected that the consideration of these issues will proceed speedily.

This analysis suggests that these issues cannot be ignored; rather, they should be taken up as priority items in the agenda of the different relevant bodies and should be handled speedily.

POSSIBLE POINTS OF WEAKNESS

There is a reference in paragraph 12 of the Declaration to paragraph 47 of the Declaration which talks about the overall balance of the negotiations in the Work Programme. This has the danger of leading to a suggestion that the solutions to the implementation issues will be included in the assessment of the overall balance in the outcome of the Work Programme. This line of suggestion will imply that the developing countries are expected to pay a price for the resolution of the implementation issues. But such an expectation is not rational, as the implementation issues have been raised by the developing countries in order to reduce the imbalances and inequities in the currently existing agreements. If they have to pay a price, these imbalances and inequities will not be reduced but will instead be perpetuated. Hence the developing countries have to guard against any such suggestion regarding inclusion of the solutions to the implementation issues in an assessment of the overall balance in the outcome of the Work Programme.

Sometimes it is argued that many of the implementation issues would entail changing the rights and obligations of WTO Members set in the agreements; as such the developed countries should not be expected to agree to them. This line of argument is not quite proper. It is true that in the normal GATT/WTO process, an obligation is not eliminated or reduced without compensation having to be paid. But the implementation issues are of a special nature. These have been identified by the developing countries as elements of deficiencies and imbalances in the system. The tackling of this problem should be considered a systemic matter, rather than as enhancement or reduction of a particular right or obligation. Further, the major developed countries have in the past extracted commitments from the developing countries on several issues in the WTO Ministerial Conferences without giving anything in return. Some examples are: the framework for zero duty on telecommunications goods in the Singapore Ministerial Conference in 1996; standstill (i.e., zero duty in practice) on duties on electronic commerce in the Geneva Ministerial Conference in May 1998; and the entry of a set of new issues into the folds of the WTO in the Singapore Ministerial Conference in 1996. The developed countries did not pay any commensurate compensation to the developing countries for the latter's agreeing to these proposals. Even going beyond the remedies for the imbalances in the Uruguay Round, the developing countries will be quite justified in asking for compensation for their having made these concessions to the major developed countries that were the main demanders in these cases.

SUGGESTED ACTION

(i)   The implementation issues will be considered in different relevant bodies in the three tracks, as mentioned above. The developing countries should try to have them placed as the first operational agenda in each of these bodies. As explained above, they will be quite justified in suggesting that these items should be taken up with high priority and speed. In fact, it will be rational to suggest that other items should be taken up in these bodies only after the consideration of the implementation issues is completed.

(ii)   These issues should form a separate ensemble in the relevant bodies and should be kept organically separated from the new issues of negotiation in these bodies in pursuance of the other parts of the Work Programme. This process is suggested to ensure that the implementation issues are not mingled with the other issues in assessing the overall balance in the results of the Work Programme.

3 AGRICULTURE (PARAS. 13, 14)

In the area of agriculture, negotiations have already been ongoing in the WTO since the beginning of 2000 in pursuance of Article 20 of the Agreement on Agriculture. They are aimed at reducing protection and support to agriculture. A number of proposals have been submitted by the Member countries during the course of the negotiations which are mainly focussed at present on working out the modalities for reduction of protection and support.

The Work Programme, in the Doha Ministerial Declaration, specifies the aim of negotiation as: substantial improvement in market access, reduction of export subsidies and substantial reduction in domestic support. Further, it intends to "enable the developing countries to effectively take account of their development needs, including food security and rural development". It lays down that special and differential treatment for the developing countries "shall be an integral part of all elements of the negotiations". It specifies that the special and differential treatment shall be "operationally effective" by embodying it in both the rules and the schedules of Members' commitments. It confirms that the non-trade concerns of the Members will be "taken into account" in the negotiations. Then it goes on to provide a time-frame for the establishment of modalities for commitments and submission of schedules.

In this manner, the Work Programme gives a particular focus and direction to the ongoing negotiations in the area of agriculture.

POINTS OF STRENGTH

(i) The aims of reduction of export subsidies "with a view to phasing (them) out" and "substantial reductions" in domestic support constitute a sound base for demands on the major developed countries for commitments in these areas. These countries have been providing huge domestic support and export subsidies in agriculture. In contrast, the levels of export subsidies in the developing countries in agriculture are negligible and those of domestic support are extremely small. Hence this aspect of the aims of negotiations can be considered to be mainly targeted at the policies and measures of the major developed countries. Apart from generally distorting trade and production in this sector, these practices of the major developed countries have been particularly harming the developing countries in two ways. The farmers of the developing countries are exposed to extremely unfair competition from such subsidized import products and stand the risk of being driven out of farming. Also, they face unfair competition in the markets of these major developed countries as well as in third-country markets where their prospects of export are unfairly curtailed by the highly subsidized products of the major developed countries.

(ii) The development needs of the developing countries, particularly for food security and rural development, have been formally recognized and targeted for action. This will enable the developing countries to have special provisions in these areas. It has been argued by the developing countries that food security, i.e., domestic production for domestic consumption, is of vital importance to them. They cannot depend on imported food as they may not always have stable reserves of foreign exchange for purchasing food in foreign markets. As for rural development, an important aspect thereof is rural employment. The rural economy of a large number of the developing countries is based on small and household farming. The vast majority of their farmers take to agriculture not as a

13

commercial venture but mainly as a traditional occupation and in the absence of any more lucrative alternative occupation. If they are faced with international competition, they will almost certainly lose out. Hence protection of the people engaged in such occupation is necessary. If they are driven out of agriculture, they are likely to be reduced to destitution, as these countries will find it extremely difficult to find alternative sources of livelihood for them. It is realistic for the Work Programme to recognize these problems and aim to find solutions for them.

(iii) Going beyond these two important concerns of the developing countries, the Work Programme has decided to make special and differential treatment for the developing countries operational by embodying it in the text of the rules and the schedules of commitments.

(iv) The "non-trade concerns" that have been mostly raised by some developed countries have been given a different and lower status. The Work Programme "take(s) note" of this item and "confirms" that these "will be taken into account" in the negotiations. The important point is that the Work Programme has drawn a distinction between the development needs of the developing countries and the non-trade concerns of some countries. It thus puts an end to the attempts made in the past, mainly by some developed countries, to mingle these two different subjects, which resulted in a great deal of confusion. Whereas in respect of the development needs, there is a definite decision to embody the solutions in the rules and schedules, in respect of the non-trade concerns, the decision is only to take them into account in the negotiations.

POSSIBLE POINTS OF WEAKNESS

(i) One of the aims of the negotiations is: "substantial reductions in trade-distorting domestic support". The qualifying term "trade-distorting" can be used by the major developed countries to suggest that the so-called "green box" domestic support, listed in Annex 2 to the Agreement on Agriculture and exempted from reduction commitments in the Uruguay Round, is not to be covered by the negotiations on reduction. But these are essentially the very subsidies that have given high and unfair advantage to the farmers in the major developed countries. Recent estimates have indicated that the total domestic support, of which the exempted categories constitute a major proportion, comes up to nearly US$360 billion per year in the developed countries. Such high domestic support has the potential of causing major damage to the domestic production and export prospects of the developing countries in the area of agriculture.

And there is no reason at all why these support measures should be exempted from reduction. Sometimes it is argued that these payments are not based on or related to production or prices; as such these should not be covered by the discipline of reduction (paragraph 6 of Annex 2 to the Agreement on Agriculture). But such a line of reasoning is faulty. After all, these payments are not made to the people in general based on some economic or social criteria, but only to the farmers from year to year, adding to their economic strength and thus helping them to continue with their uncompetitive farming. Clearly such payments are trade-distorting and help boost uncompetitive production. Hence, rather than being exempted from reduction commitments, they should be subjected to accelerated reduction and quick elimination.

(ii) It is well recognized by now that the policies and measures of the developed countries, particularly the major ones among them, are especially responsible for the distortion of agricultural trade and production. Yet, paragraph 13 of the Ministerial Declaration does not make a special reference to the policies and practices of the developed countries; rather, it makes a geographically neutral enunciation of the aims of reducing protection and subsidies. In fact, there is a danger that such a generalized statement may imply a parity between the aim of reduction of protection and subsidies in the developed countries and in the developing countries. Such ignoring of the principal focus of attention, i.e., the policies and measures of the major developed countries, is indicative of the weakness of political will of the WTO membership to tackle the basic problem in the agriculture sector.

SUGGESTED ACTION

(i)   The negotiations in this area are focusing at present on working out the modalities based on which commitments will be made by the countries and included in their respective schedules. This is the most important part of the negotiations, as the later part will mostly be an arithmetical exercise to work out the quantitative pictures based on the modalities. Hence it is of utmost importance that the developing countries play an active role in working out the modalities. A number of specific proposals have already been tabled by the developing countries. There is a need to follow them up and table additional proposals.

(ii) The developing countries should insist that the negotiations in the three areas, viz., market access, domestic support and export subsidies, must be linked together. Already the indications are that the major developed countries would like to have them considered separately and that they would like to take up the item of market access first. This poses two elements of risk. Firstly, it will shift the emphasis away from the high domestic support and export subsidies of the developed countries. Secondly, it will not provide an effective solution to the problem of trade distortion, as the best of commitments in market access by the developed countries can be almost totally nullified by weak commitments on their domestic support and export subsidies. Hence an effective integration of the negotiations in these three areas is of vital importance to the developing countries.

(iii) In sequencing the negotiations for the purposes of working out a time schedule, it has been indicated above that the major developed countries have already expressed their preference for taking up market access first. From the angle of the developing countries, it will not be a right start. They will be fully entitled to say that export subsidies, which really have no justification for existence, particularly in the developed countries, should be taken up first. Then should come domestic support and finally market access. Of course, there should be some mechanism to establish linkages in these three areas on a systemic basis and also from time to time. One effective method of linkage will be for the developing countries to make any possible offers on tariff reduction only after knowing the offers of the major developed countries on the reduction of domestic support and export subsidies.

(iv) The modalities must include the reduction of the so-called green box measures, i.e., the currently exempted support given by the developed countries.

(v) Considering that the policies and measures of the major developed countries have been the main causes of distortion of world agricultural trade and production, there is a rational ground to suggest that the work on modalities should start with at least some broad indications by the major developed countries about their possible commitments in the three areas of export subsidies, domestic support and market access. This would be a useful and necessary input into the thinking of the developing countries on their own commitments.

(vi) Some concrete suggestions should be given by the developing countries regarding how their development needs, particularly food security and rural development, are to be taken into account. Initial proposals on these elements will have to come from them. Some preliminary ideas are given below.

Food security for the developing countries essentially implies, in this connection, adequate domestic production for domestic consumption. This would imply in turn that the developing countries which have the possibility of producing adequate food should not be constrained in this regard by the current or potential disciplines of the Agreement on Agriculture. Such constraints may materialize in two ways: one, through the disciplines on import control, and two, through the disciplines on production subsidy. Thus there may be a proposal for an enabling provision that the developing countries may undertake import control measures (either through tariffs or through direct quantitative limits on imports or through a combination of the two) for protecting their domestic production for domestic consumption. Naturally a question will then arise as to how to distinguish production for domestic consumption from that for export. One simple solution will be to apply the enabling provision to the developing countries which have no export or only marginal proportion of export of food products compared to consumption.

Likewise, for rural development, particularly for the protection of rural employment, similar enabling provisions may be applied. With regard to how import control is to be linked to rural employment, a simple solution may be to apply the enabling provision to the developing countries that have a predominant proportion of small farmers among farmers as a whole. Some criteria based on the comparative size of farm holdings may be evolved.

(vii) Besides, some other solutions and criteria may also be worked out and proposed as necessary, e.g., enabling the developing countries to use the "special safeguard" provisions in the Agreement on Agriculture, or some other suggestions contained in this writer's booklet *Some Suggestions for Improvements in the WTO Agreements* (1999, Penang: Third World Network).

4 Services (Para. 15)

Negotiations in the area of services have been going on since the beginning of 2000 in pursuance of the General Agreement on Trade in Services (GATS). The Work Programme takes this process further and prescribes time schedules for requests and offers in the negotiations for liberalization in specific service sectors. An important step in the ongoing negotiations has been the adoption of the Guidelines and Procedures for the Negotiations (the Guidelines) by the Council for Trade in Services on 28 March 2001 (WTO document S/L/93 of 29 March 2001). The Work Programme reaffirms the Guidelines and also aims to achieve the objectives contained in Articles IV and XIX of the GATS. These two Articles contain specific provisions for the developing countries. The former calls for liberalization of market access in sectors and modes of supply of export interest to the developing countries. The latter provides for flexibility for the developing countries to liberalize fewer sectors and fewer transactions. It also enables them to attach conditions in specific sectors for strengthening their domestic services capacity, efficiency and competitiveness and for access to distribution channels and information networks.

The trend of the negotiations so far and the Guidelines, as also paragraph 15 of the Ministerial Declaration, indicate that the negotiations will take place on the usual basis of requests and offers in various service sectors. There is no specific recognition of the fact that the liberalization process undertaken so far has clearly been one-sided in the sense that the benefits have mainly accrued to the major developed countries, because of their enormous supply capacity in the services area. A quantitative assessment would have helped provide a clearer picture of the effects of liberalization. But the services sector does not have a proper system of relevant data. However, even in the absence of a quantitative assessment, one can draw such a qualitative conclusion based on the vast differential in the supply capacity in the area of services between the developed and the developing countries. This differential is especially pronounced in the services sectors that were taken up for accelerated negotiations, viz., financial services and telecommunication services.

Naturally the major developed countries will exert pressure for continuing with the negotiations on the pattern of the past, and thus push the developing countries into making further commitments on liberalization. This will exacerbate the imbalances in this area. There is thus a need to change the old request-and-offer type of negotiations. And it can be achieved within the mandate of the Work Programme, as will be explained shortly.

POINTS OF STRENGTH

(i)   Specific mention in paragraph 15 of the Ministerial Declaration of the aim to achieve the objectives stipulated in Articles IV and XIX of the GATS gives strength to the developing countries to pursue their goals in this area. The Guidelines, confirmed by the Declaration, ask the Council for Trade in Services to examine to what extent Article IV has been implemented and to make suggestions for promoting the implementation. All this strengthens the case of the developing countries in asking the developed countries to liberalize the sectors and modes of interest to the developing countries. It also weakens the case of the developed countries in asking for liberalization in the developing countries on a large scale.

(ii) The Guidelines specify that the existing structure and principles of the GATS shall be respected, including the Member's right to specify sectors in which commitments will be undertaken. Thus the current practice of a country choosing the sectors to come under commitments will continue. It is particularly significant as the major developed countries had tried, during the negotiations for the Guidelines, to alter this basic approach. Confirmation and retention of this principle together with the flexibility allowed to the developing countries in Article XIX as mentioned above gives them the right to choose a limited number of sectors for further commitments.

POINTS OF WEAKNESS

(i)   As mentioned above, no explicit notice has been taken of the grave imbalance in this area arising from vastly differing supply capacities. No specific method has been suggested nor guidelines given to overcome this serious deficiency.

(ii) No explicit notice has been taken of the lack of assessment of the effects of liberalization in this area. The Guidelines are also weak in this respect as they call on the Council for Trade in Services merely to continue to carry out an assessment. There is no specific sequential relationship between the assessment and further negotiations. If negotiations continue without an assessment of the effects of the liberalization so far, the developing countries will be particularly harmed.

Qualitatively, however, one can easily say that they have not got any significant gain so far because of their weak supply capacity. If they go on making commitments without first having an assessment of the current results, they will be put to further loss in the negotiations.

(iii) The Guidelines say that "the starting point for the negotiation of specific commitments shall be the current schedules, without prejudice to the content of requests". This may lead the developed countries to ignore the current imbalances in the commitments.

SUGGESTED ACTION

(i) In the current phase of placing requests and offers, the developing countries should try to invoke the flexibility permissible under Article XIX. They should draw attention to the current imbalance in the commitments because of their limited supply capacity in the service sectors liberalized in the developed countries. On this basis they will be justified in arguing that they should not be called upon to make offers of new commitments. In any case, it will be quite irrational for them to make offers of new commitments without an assessment of the effects of the current commitments.

The Guidelines say that the negotiations "shall be adjusted in the light of the results of the assessment". Of course, they refer to the new negotiations, but this spirit should also be adhered to in respect of the current balance/imbalance. If there is an imbalance at the starting point now, as is apparent at least qualitatively, the negotiations should be adjusted at the present stage so as not to enhance the imbalance. In fact, efforts should be made to eliminate or reduce the imbalance.

A point is sometimes made whether it is practical for the developing countries to take a stand that they should not be called upon to make new commitments in this area because of the existing imbalance. It should, in fact, be quite practical, as Article XIX prescribes liberalization in fewer sectors and fewer transactions. Furthermore, the Guidelines call for the examination of the implementation of Article IV. Both in substance and in strategy, it will not be proper for the developing countries to go on making offers of commitments at this stage of the negotiations without insisting on some balancing of the current asymmetric situation.

(ii) The developing countries should submit their own requests. Some of them have already identified some sectors of their interest and they should include these sectors in their requests. In this respect they should identify the constraints in the developed countries in these sectors and include them in their requests for liberalization by the developed countries. A large number of the developing countries have identified the movement of persons as an important factor in improving their export prospects in service sectors. They should therefore include this mode of supply in these sectors in their requests for liberalization in the developed countries.

(iii) The ongoing work in the area of recognition (Article VII of the GATS) has an important bearing on the utilization of the opportunities provided by the market access commitments made by others. By now, the developing countries have some experience of the actual situation in this area in the major developed countries. Hence the evaluation of the offers of the developed countries should be made in the light of the relevant recognition rules and practices in those countries. The developing countries should also keep it in view while preparing the requests to be made to the developed countries.

(iv) For operationalizing Article IV, some specific suggestions have been given in this writer's booklet, *Some Suggestions for Improvements in the WTO Agreements*, referred to earlier.

5 MARKET ACCESS FOR NON-AGRICULTURAL PRODUCTS (PARA. 16)

Paragraph 16 of the Ministerial Declaration launches negotiations in the area of market access for non-agricultural products. Though non-tariff barriers have also been included for negotiation, the exercise will mainly focus on industrial tariffs. The aim of the negotiations is to reduce industrial tariffs. Tariff peaks, high tariffs and tariff escalation have also been specifically identified as targets for reduction. The stipulation is that the product coverage shall be comprehensive, which means that the negotiations will not be limited to any particular areas. Also, the paragraph says that no area will be excluded *a priori*. All this makes the negotiations on industrial tariffs a massive exercise similar to the tariff negotiations in recent rounds of multilateral trade negotiations.

It is likely that some formulae may be worked out for general reduction of industrial tariffs. Usually the formulae include criteria for maximum tariffs, average tariff targets, pace of reduction, etc. Side by side, there may also be some bilateral exercises for reduction of tariffs on specific products of interest to specific countries.

Compared to the previous tariff reduction exercises, the current one has deeper implications for the developing countries. It could adversely affect the process of industrialization and upgradation of industries. As direct import control measures have been almost totally abolished in the developing countries (the major developed countries still maintain some direct import control measures, e.g., in the textiles sector) and as the balance-of-payments measures under Article XVIIIB of the GATT 1994 have been put under severe discipline, tariffs are practically the only instrument of protection in the industrial sector. Indiscriminate lowering of industrial tariffs in the developing countries can impede industrialization and upgradation of industries and can even lead to de-industrialization. Some recent studies have brought to light the adverse effects of rapid reduction of industrial tariffs on the industrial development of African countries. Hence it is imperative that the negotiations for the reduction of industrial tariffs should be approached and handled by the developing countries with great care.

POINTS OF STRENGTH

(i) The Work Programme aims at reducing tariffs, "in particular" on products of export interest to the developing countries. Hence even though there is a stipulation of comprehensive product coverage in the paragraph, the products of export interest to the developing countries have to be given special attention. The major developed countries have high tariffs on such products compared to their tariffs on other products. Hence it will be rational for the developing countries to argue that the developed countries should especially lower their tariffs on such products.

(ii) The paragraph says that the negotiations "shall take fully into account the special needs and interests of developing and least-developed country participants". In actual operation, it will have two tracks of implementation, viz., one, the developed countries will be required to make substantial reductions in the tariffs on the products of export interest to the developing countries, including the least developed countries, and two, the developing countries, including the least developed countries, on the other hand, will not be required to have coverage of products and depth of tariff cuts that may be detrimental to their development needs.

(iii) The paragraph goes on to say that there will be "less than full" reciprocity in the reduction commitments by the developing countries, including the least developed countries. Though the term "less than full" does not specify quantitatively what should be the relative expectation of reduction from the developing countries, the direction and approach in the reduction is clear from such a stipulation.

(iv) The tariff reduction exercise will be based on "modalities to be agreed". Hence the first task in the negotiating process will be to work out the modalities. The developing countries will have the opportunity to include their special concerns at this stage of the negotiations right in the beginning.

POSSIBLE POINTS OF WEAKNESS

(i) The main targets in this exercise of tariff reduction will be the developing countries. The developed countries have low average industrial tariffs, though the tariffs on some individual items (particularly on the products of export interest to the developing countries) are relatively high. A large number of the developing countries have comparatively higher average industrial tariffs, because of the need for protection of their industries and other development needs. Hence the developing countries are particularly vulnerable in this area of negotiation. However, the qualifications mentioned in this paragraph as indicated above may afford them some defensive strength.

(ii) There may be a tendency to work out the formulae for the reduction based on past practices. This may be harmful to the developing countries. Hence some new alternative formulae should be evolved. Some suggestions on this point are given below.

SUGGESTED ACTION

(i)   There should be a detailed and comprehensive exercise right in the beginning for working out the modalities for tariff reduction. The modalities should include: identification of products of export interest to the developing countries, including the least developed countries, the manner of giving them special consideration in tariff reduction in the developed countries, identification of tariff peaks and tariff escalation in the developed countries, the manner of eliminating or substantially reducing them, elucidation of special needs and interests of developing countries including the least developed countries in respect of their own tariffs and tariff structure, elucidation and operationalization of the concept of "less than full reciprocity", studies to assess the impact of earlier tariff reduction exercises on the developing countries' industrialization and development, studies to assess the possible potential impact of future tariff reduction on industrialization and development, etc. Negotiations should be undertaken on tariff reduction only after the modalities have been fully worked out.

(ii)   Before working out the formulae for general tariff reduction, an exercise should be undertaken on a priority basis for the elimination or substantial reduction of tariff peaks, high tariffs and tariff escalation in the developed countries. The modalities mentioned above will help in this process. There is justification for attending to this problem on a priority basis as the Declaration itself lays particular emphasis on it. It will be proper to separate out the tariff peaks, high tariffs and tariff escalation in the developed countries from the general tariff reduction exercise and address them for solution before attending to general tariff reduction.

(iii) While working out the formulae for general tariff reduction, the differences in the current structure of tariffs in the developed and the developing countries should be kept in view by the developing countries. The average industrial tariff is comparatively low in the developed countries and generally comparatively high in the developing countries. Given such a tariff structure, it is prudent for the developing countries to have a formula that reduces the gap between the average tariff and the higher tariffs, rather than having a formula which primarily aims at reducing the average tariff. Moreover, the highest permissible tariff level should not be indicated as a specific number; it should instead be prescribed as a specified multiple of the average tariff.

6 TRIPS (Paras. 17, 18, 19)

The provisions of the Work Programme relating to trade-related aspects of intellectual property rights (TRIPS) are contained in paragraphs 17,18 and 19 of the Declaration and also in the Ministerial Declaration on the TRIPS Agreement and Public Health [WTO document WT/MIN(01)/DEC/W/2 of 14 November 2001].

The Work Programme envisages: (i) negotiations on establishment of a multilateral system of notification and registration of geographical indications for wines and spirits, (ii) examination of the relationship between the TRIPS Agreement and the Convention on Biological Diversity, (iii) examination of protection of traditional knowledge and folklore, and (iv) finding an expeditious solution in the TRIPS Council to the problems faced by countries with insufficient manufacturing capacity in the pharmaceutical sector in effectively invoking the provision in the TRIPS Agreement on compulsory licensing.

There are nine proposals on TRIPS under the heading of "implementation issues" contained in items 87 to 95 of the General Council document of 20 February 2001 referred to above [JOB(01)/14].

Apart from all these items specifically mentioned in the Work Programme, the ongoing work will continue on the review of Article 27.3(b) of the TRIPS Agreement and the review of the implementation of the Agreement as mandated in Article 71.1. Already some proposals have been made by the developing countries on Article 27.3(b).

The developing countries have been quite active in this area and also very well prepared. The follow-up of the Work Programme has already started in the TRIPS Council with the proposals and discussions on the problems of countries relating to compulsory licensing in the pharmaceutical sector. The developing countries have already placed some proposals in the Council.

SUGGESTED ACTION

(i)   The Declaration on TRIPS and Public Health contains some important elements which the developing countries should build on. Paragraph 4 says that the TRIPS Agreement "can and should be" interpreted and implemented in a manner that is supportive of the rights of countries to promote access to medicines to all and to protect public health in general. It is a guiding principle, but by itself it does not give interpretations of the relevant provisions in the TRIPS Agreement. It is very uncertain how the developed countries will implement it or be guided by it. It is also uncertain how the panels and the Appellate Body in the WTO's dispute settlement mechanism will use it for their interpretation exercise whenever needed. It is desirable that the developing countries take the lead and identify some specific points for interpretation and place such specific proposals of interpretation in the TRIPS Council, which will send them to the General Council with its recommendations.

(ii) As mentioned above, the developing countries have placed some proposals regarding use of compulsory licensing for pharmaceutical products in countries with insufficient manufacturing capacity. They have also impressed on the major developed countries that their proposals are in accordance with paragraph 4 of the Declaration on TRIPS and Public Health mentioned above. It will be useful to pursue this line and see if the major developed countries are willing to respect the letter and spirit of this provision of the Declaration.

(iii) The proposals of the developing countries in connection with Article 27.3(b) of the TRIPS Agreement should naturally be pursued. In fact there can be a continuing process of identifying issues and placing proposals on this matter and other relevant matters. The review process has already started. The TRIPS Agreement does not prescribe any time limit for closing this review.

The implementation review as required in Article 71.1 should have started in 2000, and thereafter been undertaken every two years. But this review has not been taken up effectively. The developing countries should take the lead and place proposals for this review. There need be no sequencing of the two reviews, viz., the one under Article 27.3(b) and the other under Article 71.1. Both should be undertaken together, so that the developing countries are able to table their proposals in a comprehensive manner.

Some suggestions have been given in this writer's booklet *Some Suggestions for Improvements in the WTO Agreements* referred to earlier, which can be used by the developing countries in formulating their proposals.

7 RELATIONSHIP BETWEEN TRADE AND INVESTMENT (PARAS. 20, 21, 22)

RELATED PART OF DECLARATION AND CHAIRMAN'S STATEMENT

This is one of the four Singapore issues (called thus because these four subjects entered the WTO frame in the First Ministerial Conference of the WTO held in Singapore in November-December 1996). The other three issues are competition policy, transparency in government procurement and trade facilitation, which will be dealt with in later chapters. The decisions on negotiations in each of these four areas taken in the Fourth Ministerial Conference in Doha are similar. As there has been some controversy on the exact content of the decisions, it is examined in the next few paragraphs in detail. This analysis is applicable to all the four Singapore issues.

The relevant sentence in the Ministerial Declaration and a related statement by the Chairman of the Doha Ministerial Conference should be considered together in examining this matter. In the Declaration, it is "agree(d) that negotiations will take place after the Fifth Session of the Ministerial Conference on the basis of a decision to be taken, by explicit consensus, at that Session on modalities of negotiations". This provision appears in the respective sections of the Declaration dealing with each of the four Singapore issues (viz., paragraphs 20, 23, 26 and 27). Then there was a statement made by the Chairman of the Conference, Mr Youssef Hussain Kamal, the Qatari Minister of Finance, Economy and Trade, at its closing plenary session on 14 November 2001, which is quoted below:

"I would like to note that some delegations have requested clarification concerning Paragraphs 20, 23, 26 and 27 of the draft declaration. Let me say that with respect to the reference to an 'explicit consensus' being needed, in these paragraphs, for a decision to be taken at the Fifth Session of the Ministerial Conference, my understanding is that, at that session, a decision would indeed need to be taken by explicit consensus, before negotiations on trade and investment and trade and competition policy, transparency in government procurement, and trade facilitation could proceed.

"In my view, this would also give each member the right to take a position on modalities that would prevent negotiations from proceeding after the Fifth Session of the Ministerial Conference until that member is prepared to join in an explicit consensus."

The Chairman made this statement in response to the requests of some delegations for "clarification concerning Paragraphs 20, 23, 26 and 27". Hence his statement is in the nature of a "clarification" of the language in these paragraphs. Also the Chairman has termed the first part of his statement "(his) understanding". Normally a chairman arrives at such understanding by a process of consultations with the participants in the meeting and he/she includes agreed formulations in his/her understanding. If there is no objection or reservation from the participants after the chairman has expressed his/her understanding, it is considered to be the collective wish of the meeting. In this plenary during this Conference, there was no objection or reservation from the participants after the Chairman expressed his understanding. All this makes this part binding on the WTO process unless it is modified by a later WTO Ministerial Conference.

This part of his statement will be considered to interpret the meaning of the language in these paragraphs (i.e., paragraphs 20, 23, 26 and 27). Hence it is necessary to have an explicit consensus before negotiations in these four respective areas "could proceed". The text in the relevant paragraphs in the Declaration speaks about a decision by explicit consensus on modalities of negotiations. A question arises as to whether the negotiations will automatically proceed when the modalities are agreed to by explicit consensus. Here the text in the Chairman's statement comes into play. It speaks about a decision by explicit consensus for the negotiations to proceed. All this considered together suggests a two-stage decision by explicit consensus: one stage for the modalities of negotiations and another stage for the negotiations to proceed. It should be noted that there is no prescribed sequencing in these two stages; for example, even before the modalities are taken up for a decision (by explicit consensus), the matter of negotiations itself can be taken up for decision (by explicit consensus).

Decision by consensus is defined in footnote 1 to Article IX of the Marrakesh Agreement Establishing the WTO as a situation when "no Member, present at the meeting when the decision is taken, formally objects to the proposed decision". Thus, technically speaking, even one Member can withhold consensus on modalities and thereby withhold the negotiations in this area. Also even one Member can withhold consensus for negotiations to proceed.

In actual practice, how this will play out will depend on the motivation of the Members and the political situation prevailing at the relevant time. The Fifth Ministerial Conference will be technically within its rights to alter the situation created by this understanding.

WORK UP TO FIFTH MINISTERIAL CONFERENCE

The Working Group on the Relationship Between Trade and Investment has been examining this relationship since 1996. Now the Declaration says that the Working Group will, in the period leading up to the Fifth Ministerial Conference, focus on certain specific elements. Besides, as mentioned in paragraph 20 of the Declaration and also in the statement of the Chairman, "modalities of negotiations" will be worked out. What will be the essential subjects of the "modalities" has not been spelt out.

The Declaration is silent on this point.

Paragraph 22 of the Declaration asks the Working Group to focus on the clarification of certain elements, viz., (i) scope and definition, (ii) transparency, (iii) non-discrimination, (iv) modalities for pre-establishment commitments based on GATS-type positive-list approach, (v) development provisions, (vi) exceptions and balance-of-payments safeguards, and (vii) consultation and dispute settlement.

Then the Declaration goes on to give some guidelines on a possible framework on investment, e.g., the framework should reflect balanced interests of home and host countries, take account of development policies and development objectives of the host governments, take into account the special development, trade and financial needs of developing countries including the least developed countries, etc. It should be noted that these are the guidelines for a "framework", and negotiations on the "framework" can take place only after the Fifth Ministerial Conference, if the conditions mentioned above are fulfilled. Hence the relevance of these guidelines to the current work of the Working Group is not clear.

SUGGESTED ACTION

Background

The objective of the proponents of investment negotiations in the WTO is to ensure and strengthen the protection of the rights of foreign investors in host countries and to curtail the role of the host government in putting conditions on foreign investors' entry and operation. This has serious implications for the developing countries. They have priorities of development and would like to channel foreign investment to the priority areas, for example, in building of infrastructure, in production of exportable goods and services and in sectors which will instill innate strength to the country's economy. They would also like to have a proper geographical spread of the foreign investment so that the underdeveloped regions of the country get priority attention. Further, they will prefer that the operation of the foreign investment is carried out in such a way that it links with domestic economic activity in a positive manner with mutual benefit to both the foreign investor and the domestic economic activities. They will be keen to guard against any adverse effects of the foreign investment on their economic, social and political process. The realization of all these objectives needs concrete government policies and measures.

The objective of the proponents of this subject in the WTO, however, is to restrict the policy options available to the government in this regard so that the investor has freedom of entry and operation. It can have serious adverse impact on the host country's economy and its economic structure. The developing countries are particularly vulnerable in this regard. Hence it is quite natural that a large number of them have been extremely reluctant to let this issue enter the WTO, where binding commitments cannot be annulled or modified without giving commensurate compensation. The approach of the developing countries to the work in the Working Group should be guided by these real apprehensions.

Elements for clarification included in paragraph 22 of the Declaration

The Work Programme, as mentioned above, has identified certain elements for clarification as the focus of the work. Two important points need to be emphasized here. Firstly, the items are mentioned for "clarification". Thus the existence of an item here does not mean that it has already been accepted as an appropriate subject in a multilateral framework on investment. After the clarification exercise, it may be decided that the item should be treated in a certain way or that it should not be included at all. Secondly, it should be noted that these are not exclusive elements for clarification, since these have been identified for the focus of the work and not as exclusive work. Hence this paragraph of the Declaration does not prevent the developing countries from identifying some other elements for consideration or clarification. In fact, it will be useful if the developing countries, apart from giving their ideas on these stated elements, also put forward some other elements which they consider important from their point of view.

Doubts may arise as to whether the developing countries should actively engage in this exercise as they have been objecting to an expansion of the work on investment in the WTO. However, it is important for them to engage fully in this exercise at this stage; otherwise the work on clarification of these elements will go on without their contribution and they will thus lose an opportunity to place their ideas on the table and have an effective say in determining the content and relevance of these elements. The advantage for them lies in active participation and placing other elements for clarification which they may consider relevant.

Some preliminary ideas are given below in respect of the points for clarification identified as the focus of work in the Work Programme.

Scope and definition

Considering that this whole exercise is aimed at curtailing the government's options and role, it is important for the developing countries to have the scope and definition formulated in such a way that it is limited, well defined and not amenable to future expansion. For example, it is desirable to limit the scope to foreign direct investment (FDI), excluding portfolio investment, loans or credit, short-term deposits, speculative funds and other such flows of funds. It should be ensured that the definition of FDI is fully clear and totally unambiguous.

Transparency

Transparency should be limited to automatic or easy availability of the relevant rules, procedures and decisions. It should not transgress into the area of the substantive decision-making process.

Non-discrimination

Non-discrimination has two elements, viz., one, non-discrimination as between the investors of the territories of different Members (most-favoured-nation (MFN) principle) and two, non-discrimination as between the foreign investor and domestic investor (national-treatment principle). Both these principles are dangerous in respect of the developing countries; and, between the two, the second is much more dangerous. Developing countries should have the flexibility to give preference to investments from particular countries, based on past experience and past linkages as also on the perception of future trends of cooperation. It will be extremely harmful for the developing countries to include national treatment, i.e., non-discrimination as between the foreign investor and domestic investor, in a possible framework for investment. Domestic investors stand on a different footing altogether. For example, they do not repatriate the returns on investment to foreign countries, they are more inclined to have domestic linkages with their investment, thus generating further domestic economic activities, etc.

It will not be enough if the developing countries are given some differential treatment in this respect. Past experience in the GATT/WTO system has shown that differential treatment does not offer the safeguard of real and stable protection. What should be ensured is that the principle of non-discrimination as seen in the WTO sense, as explained above, should have absolutely no place in a framework for investment.

Modalities for pre-establishment commitments based on GATS-type positive-list approach

Here the reference is to the specific commitments in the GATS: under that agreement, a country chooses which service sector to include in its schedule of commitments and what conditions to apply on the entry and operation of foreign service suppliers. In the context of investment, this approach would perhaps imply that a country will undertake obligations on the entry of investment only in areas specified by it and also will be able to prescribe conditions on entry and operation.

On the surface this may appear safe. But the experience with the GATS negotiations on specific commitments has shown that it does not give adequate protection to the developing countries. Though in theory a country may be free to choose sectors for inclusion in its schedule of commitments, in actual practice, its commitments, including its choice of sectors, will be the result of a series of bilateral and plurilateral negotiations with other countries, in particular the major developed countries. In these negotiations, individual developing countries are subjected to intense pressures from the major developed countries and are often unable to limit their commitments to the sectors of their choice.

Development provisions

A desirable development provision will be that a developing country will be totally free to apply conditions on the entry and operation of the FDI in accordance with its own perception and decision on its development process. A developing country should have total freedom to make its own autonomous decision and thus should not be required to justify it either bilaterally or multilaterally.

Also, a developing country should be enabled to apply the domestic-content requirement, which is at present prohibited under the Agreement on Trade-Related Investment Measures (TRIMs) and Article III of the GATT 1994. This requirement obliges investors to use at least a specified minimum amount of local inputs.

Exceptions and balance-of-payments safeguards

If a developing country has full discretion and flexibility in relation to putting conditions on the entry and operation of FDI, it will not need exceptions and balance-of-payments safeguards. While allowing the entry of investment it will be retaining its policy options in the situations needing exceptions or balance-of-payments safeguards.

Consultation and dispute settlement between Members

A possible framework will have a dispute settlement process to resolve disputes between the Members. The investors should have no role in this process. The dispute settlement mechanism should be separated from the normal Dispute Settlement Understanding (DSU) of the WTO, in the sense that there should be no provision of cross-retaliation as is contained in Article 22.3 of the DSU.

Elements for clarification to be placed by the developing countries

As mentioned earlier, these are not the exclusive elements for clarification. Surprisingly, the selection of these elements has been very much one-sided. Several specific points made by the developing countries in the Working Group which could have formed part of this list of elements have not been taken into account. Hence it is important for the developing countries to place their own points for clarification in this part of the work of the Working Group. Some proposals of this nature had been included by the developing countries in the draft Ministerial Declaration for the 1999 Seattle Ministerial Conference (paragraph 56 of that draft). Suggestions are given below for some elements to be introduced by the developing countries in the Working Group.

Obligations of foreign investors

The foreign investors should have the obligation not to undertake what are considered restrictive business practices, e.g., restrictive conditions on consumers or other users, transfer pricing, collusive pricing, predatory practices, etc. They should also have the specific obligation of total transparency in their dealings, particularly in respect of their raising of resources, sale of products and services, purchase of products and services, distribution and use of profits, etc. Further they should be prohibited from acting in a manner that is prejudicial to the social norms and economic interests of the host country. There should be a provision for international blacklisting of the investors found to be defaulting on their obligations.

Foreign investors may also be obliged to: undertake technology transfer (including to domestic firms), train domestic personnel, allow domestic firms/persons participation in equity, bring specified amounts of capital, retain certain levels of profit in the country, etc.

Obligations of home government

The home government of the foreign investor should have the obligation to ensure that the obligations of the foreign investor are fully discharged.

These are only some examples of elements which the developing countries may bring up for clarification in the Working Group. There may be other elements based on the experiences of the developing countries with foreign investment over the years.

8 INTERACTION BETWEEN TRADE AND COMPETITION POLICY (PARAS. 23, 24, 25)

The explanation of the status of the decision on negotiations provided in the preceding chapter on investment applies to the subject of competition policy too.

BACKGROUND

The objective of the proponents of this subject in the WTO is to provide full freedom of operation for their trading firms in other countries, particularly the developing countries. They argue that foreign firms should have effective equality of opportunity as domestic firms in the domestic market. This is really the crux of their approach to competition policy in the WTO context. Towards this end their aim is to curtail the discretion and flexibility of the host government to guide the entry and operation of foreign firms and to prohibit the enjoyment of any special advantage by the domestic firms. For example, a developing country may like to give special treatment to its domestic trading firms in the matter of taxation, use of domestic distribution channels, etc., while denying these advantages to the foreign trading firms. The proponents of the Singapore issues in the WTO would particularly target these and other similar flexibilities available to the governments at present. The developing countries have been opposing the entry of this subject in the WTO, as, among other reasons, they feel that it will expose their own domestic firms to intense competition from the big multinational foreign firms in the domestic market.

Competition policy is an integral element of the development policy of the developing countries. The experience of some developed countries indicates that they have modulated their competition policy over the years to suit prevailing conditions at various stages of their development. It is prudent for the developing countries to do likewise. Therefore, if they lose their flexibility and options in respect of their competition policy, it will operate against their process of development. The intention of the proponents of this subject in the WTO implies precisely this loss of flexibility and options. The work in the Working Group on the Interaction Between Trade and Competition Policy until the Fifth Ministerial Conference should be approached in this context.

ELEMENTS FOR CLARIFICATION INCLUDED IN PARAGRAPH 25

The Work Programme, in paragraph 25 of the Ministerial Declaration, specifies some elements for clarification in the Working Group on competition policy in the period until the Fifth Ministerial Conference. As in the case of investment, these are not in the nature of exclusive elements. Consideration of other elements is not prohibited. Hence the developing countries should place some other elements of importance to them for clarification. Also, as explained in the chapter on investment, the inclusion of these elements for clarification does not imply accepting them in any possible framework.

The question of whether the developing countries should engage in the exercise of clarification of these elements has been discussed in the chapter on investment and the suggestion made there applies to this subject too.

Some brief comments are given below on the elements mentioned in paragraph 25.

Transparency, non-discrimination

The comments given on these elements above in the chapter on investment are applicable here too.

Procedural fairness, provisions on hardcore cartels

The content of these elements is not clear. Perhaps these elements have been derived from the practices of the major developed countries, as has often been the case with the framing of rules in the GATT/WTO system. The developing countries may seek clarification from the relevant countries on the exact content of these elements and prepare their position accordingly.

Modalities for voluntary cooperation

This element is also not quite clear. Clarification may be sought by the developing countries from the major developed countries which have provisions for voluntary cooperation, and responses may be prepared based on the information.

ELEMENTS TO BE PROPOSED BY DEVELOPING COUNTRIES

As suggested above in the chapter on investment, the developing countries should formulate their own proposals for additional elements for clarification in the Working Group. Some suggestions are given below.

Obligations of the firms

The suggestions given above in the chapter on investment are applicable here too. All those elements may be included in this subject as well.

Obligation of home government

The suggestions given above in the chapter on investment are applicable here too. All those elements may be included in this subject as well.

Competitiveness of domestic firms

In the context of rapid liberalization in the domestic and external economic environment, maintaining and enhancing the competitiveness of domestic firms, particularly small firms, becomes a challenging task. It is important to consider the relevant measures to be undertaken by the domestic firms, by the government and by a possible multilateral framework in this regard.

Competition impeded by government action

Government policies and measures which directly or indirectly impede competition should be included in the list for clarification. For example, anti-dumping actions should be considered, as has been proposed by the developing countries in the past.

Competition impeded by intellectual property protection

The protection of intellectual property by giving exclusive monopoly rights to the intellectual property holders results in severe limitation to competition. It severely limits production and sale.

Global monopolies and oligopolies

In several areas and sectors of production, there are only a small number of producers and/or traders. This results in a monopoly or near-monopoly situation in the world market in that sector.

Big mergers and acquisitions

Almost every day the economic journals feature some news about corporate mega-mergers. Such mergers impede competition. This issue should be an important element for inclusion in the role of a possible multilateral framework on competition.

These are only some examples of elements on which clarification may be sought in the Working Group. The developing countries may identify other elements based on their experiences over the years.

9 TRANSPARENCY IN GOVERNMENT PROCUREMENT (PARA. 26)

The explanation in the chapter on investment of the decision regarding negotiations applies to this subject also.

The work in the Working Group on Transparency in Government Procurement until the Fifth Ministerial Conference will continue on the elements of an agreement thereon and on the modalities of negotiations for an agreement. There is a specific commitment in paragraph 26 of the Ministerial Declaration that the negotiations must be "limited to the transparency aspects and therefore will not restrict the scope for countries to give preferences to domestic supplies and suppliers".

BACKGROUND

The subject of government procurement was introduced by the major developed countries primarily to gain access of supply to the market in foreign government purchases, particularly in the developing countries. Governments currently have flexibility and options in these purchases regarding the source of supply.

Government procurement, i.e., purchases for the use of the government, is not covered at present by the rules of MFN and national treatment. Hence a country can accord preference to supplies from a particular country over those from another. Also, a country can prefer supplies from domestic suppliers to the supplies from foreign suppliers. These flexibilities and options are very important for the developing countries.

Government procurement forms a sizeable market in many developing countries. They can use it as a lever to get some advantage in a foreign country. More importantly, they can use it to encourage domestic production. Hence it is important for them that these rights are retained by the government. But the major developed countries have been viewing it as an obstacle to the expansion of their market opportunities in the developing countries.

There is a WTO plurilateral agreement on government procurement of which just a couple of the developing countries are members. The rest are out of it, because they would like to retain their flexibility and options for the purposes mentioned above.

The developing countries severely opposed any attempt to start negotiations on an agreement which would cover the area of market access in government procurement. The major developed countries then lowered their target and proposed working out elements for an agreement on "transparency in government procurement." This was agreed in the Singapore Ministerial Conference in 1996.

SUGGESTED ACTION

The Working Group will be continuing with its work on the elements for a possible agreement on transparency in government procurement. The developing countries have been actively participating in this exercise. They should continue to do so. They should ensure in this process that: (i) the elements of a possible multilateral agreement on transparency in government procurement do not overburden the government machinery entrusted with the task of government procurement, and (ii) the exercise does not in any way transgress into the area of market access. The relevant paragraph of the Declaration already reaffirms, as mentioned above, that possible future negotiations in this area must be limited to transparency. Transparency means automatic and easy availability of information on the rules and practices and also the final decisions. It may also cover easy availability of information on tenders and specifications of products to be procured. It must not include the areas of evaluation of offers, decision-making process and relief to the unsuccessful tenderers, as these are elements of substantial decisions and not transparency.

During the work in the Working Group in 1999, some major developed countries had placed proposals in this area which went much beyond transparency and tried to cover the area of decision-making. Such efforts should be resisted.

Whatever provisions are worked out for transparency in government procurement should be applicable only as guiding principles or best-endeavour provisions not enforceable through the dispute settlement process.

10 TRADE FACILITATION (PARA. 27)

The analysis of the decision regarding negotiations in the chapter on investment applies to the subject of trade facilitation as well.

BACKGROUND

The work in this area until the Fifth Ministerial Conference will be conducted in the Council for Trade in Goods. This work will be on review, clarification and improvement of Articles V (freedom of transit), VIII (fees and formalities connected with import and export) and X (publication and administration of trade regulations) of the GATT 1994.

This subject, coming at the residual end of the Singapore issues, has not received much serious attention from the developing countries. It should be realized, however, that there are grave dangers involved in potential agreements in this area if the proposals of the proponents are incorporated in the form of binding commitments. The main objective of the proponents is to have the developing countries adopt rules and procedures in this area which are similar to theirs. It ignores the wide difference in the level of administrative, financial and human resources between the developed countries and developing countries. Also it does not give weightage to the wide difference in social and working environments.

For example, one set of proposals would like to have physical examinations of goods by customs authorities only in a small number of cases selected on a random basis. While this will improve the flow of goods through the customs barrier, it will also increase the risk of avoidance of payment of adequate customs duties. Such a practice may be appropriate for the major developed countries where the probability of leakage is negligible, but it may not be appropriate for the developing countries where leakage is higher.

Clarification and improvement of the rules in this area will add to the commitments of the developing countries in the WTO. For the developed countries too, there will be commitments, but it may not be as burdensome for them as most of them are already following these practices. For the developing countries, on the other hand, it may add new burdens and may have adverse implications too, as illustrated in the example given above.

SUGGESTED ACTION

The negotiating structure of the developing countries should be in close contact with the administrative machinery involved in these areas. Inputs based on the latter's experience should be given high weightage in determining negotiating positions on assuming new commitments. Past experience has shown that the administrative machinery in the developing countries often finds it difficult to implement the commitments made in the GATT/WTO.

During the negotiations, it should be emphasized that in these areas it will be more proper and practical to have national efforts, aided by technical assistance, to bring about improvement, rather than impose obligations through additional commitments in the WTO.

If the consideration of the problems in these areas results in some solutions, these should, at best, be adopted only as guiding principles or as flexible best-endeavour provisions not enforceable through the dispute settlement process.

11 WTO Rules and Dispute Settlement (Paras. 28, 29, 30)

Paragraph 28 of the Ministerial Declaration launches negotiations on subsidies and anti-dumping, paragraph 29 on regional trading arrangements (RTAs) and paragraph 30 on dispute settlement. The negotiations on subsidies and anti-dumping are aimed at clarifying and improving the disciplines in these respective areas. The negotiations in the area of RTAs are aimed at clarifying and improving the WTO disciplines and procedures which apply to such arrangements. The negotiations in the area of dispute settlement are aimed at clarifying and improving the Dispute Settlement Understanding. The scope of negotiations in all these areas extends to clarification and improvement. Clarification involves interpretation, whereas improvement may involve amendment. Hence this part of the Work Programme envisages comprehensive negotiations in these areas involving rights and obligations and may even involve reopening of some of the provisions. Paragraph 28 puts in a qualification in respect of subsidies and anti-dumping to the effect that the basic concepts, principles and effectiveness of the respective agreements and their instruments and objectives will remain preserved in the negotiations.

Clarification may be necessary when there is, for example, a case of differing interpretations or the existence of a range of options which needs to be narrowed down or widely differing permissible practices needing harmonization. Improvement may be called for when the implementation of some provision has been creating serious difficulties or when the existence of some provision is considered to be improper. It should be noted that "improving disciplines" does not necessarily imply enhancing the discipline; it may even mean lowering the level of discipline in some cases, depending on the objectives to be achieved.

POINTS OF STRENGTH

The comprehensive negotiations in these areas provide an opportunity to the developing countries to eliminate or substantially reduce the imbalances in the rules thereon and also eliminate or substantially reduce the harassment of the developing countries arising out of the operation of some of these rules in the developed countries. There need be no hesitation in making proposals for amendment of the provisions which have proved to be iniquitous or irksome. The qualifying clause in paragraph 28 in respect of subsidies and anti-dumping does not prevent consideration of proposals for amendments of the rules. The developing countries have been complaining for some years about the deficiencies, imbalances and iniquities in these agreements. Now an occasion has come when they can place their proposals for changes in these agreements to their advantage.

POINTS OF WEAKNESS

The qualifying clause in paragraph 28 about preserving the basic concepts, principles and effectiveness of the agreements on subsidies and anti-dumping may be used by the major developed countries to resist consideration of proposals for improvement of the agreements. But such efforts by them will not be logical. For example, in the area of subsidies, the basic concepts and principles are that domestic production should not be injured by unfair trade aided by subsidies and if there is such trade, the importing country has the right to introduce correctives in the form of additional duties. This should in no way prevent the consideration of proposals for elimination of defects and deficiencies in determining the amount of subsidy and existence of injury.

The major developed countries may try to limit the use of these paragraphs to bringing about small changes in the procedures in these areas. But the Work Programme set out in these paragraphs does not call for such limitation. Hence, such restrictive moves can be easily defeated, if the developing countries are prepared with their substantial proposals for improvement of these agreements.

There may be a lurking fear among some developing countries that the unravelling of these agreements may not be safe for them, as it may result in still more unfair results in the negotiations. But this fear may not be quite material. If they have found some parts of these agreements to be operating against their interests, there should be no hesitation in presenting proposals for correcting the situation. And in these areas, a large number of the developing countries may have some commonly shared experiences which may inspire them to forge a common and joint approach. This will reduce the danger of the final results going against their interests.

SUGGESTED ACTION

The main exercise in these areas of the Work Programme for the developing countries will be to prepare their proposals and place them in the appropriate negotiating bodies. Already a lot of work has been done by them in the last three years. They may pool all this work for the purpose of preparing their proposals and the arguments to back up the proposals. Some suggestions in this regard are given below.

A large number of the developing-country proposals have already been included under the heading of "implementation issues". These are contained in the General Council document of 20 February 2001 referred to in the chapter on implementation issues, i.e., JOB(01)/14. There are 15 proposals (serials 41 to 55) on anti-dumping and 20 proposals (serials 64 to 83) on subsidies. These proposals may be included in the exercise of clarification and improvement of these two agreements.

Another source of proposals in the areas of subsidies, anti-dumping and dispute settlement is this writer's booklet *Some Suggestions for Improvements in the WTO Agreements*, referred to earlier. This booklet gives eight suggestions in the areas of subsidies and anti-dumping and six suggestions in the area of dispute settlement. The developing countries may consider these suggestions while making their proposals.

Besides, the developing countries have their own experience of the workings of these agreements for nearly seven years. These experiences may be drawn upon as the basis for preparing new proposals.

In the area of RTAs, there is only one proposal (serial 98) under the heading of implementation issues in the General Council document of 20 February 2001 referred to above. This proposal is about granting waivers to RTAs between developed and developing countries. Other proposals based on the experiences of the developing countries may be prepared. Some important elements which may be covered by their proposals are the following:

(i)   RTAs among the developed countries must not reduce the market access of the developing countries in those developed countries. The related existing provision in Article XXIV.4 and Article XXIV.5(a) of the GATT 1994 needs to be refined and specified in relation to the effect on the developing countries. In fact, the burden of proof should be on the developed-country members of the RTA to demonstrate that the market access of the developing countries has not been reduced.

(ii) Where the developing countries form RTAs among themselves, there should be flexibility in relation to the coverage of trade by the agreement. Towards that end, the provision in Article XXIV regarding elimination of duties and other restrictions with respect to "substantially all the trade" between the members of the RTA should be relaxed.

The developing countries are in the process of preparing proposals while learning from their experience. Also they do not have the type of support and resources which the developed countries have. Hence the programme of work in the negotiating bodies should not put an early embargo on new proposals from the developing countries.

12 TRADE AND ENVIRONMENT (PARAS. 31, 32)

This is a new area of negotiation included in the WTO as a part of the Work Programme. The provisions on environment are contained in paragraphs 31 and 32 of the Ministerial Declaration. Paragraph 31 launches negotiations on the relationship between WTO rules and specific trade obligations in multilateral environment agreements (MEAs), and on the reduction of tariff and non-tariff barriers to environmental goods and services. The procedure for information exchange between MEA secretariats and WTO committees will also be negotiated.

Paragraph 32 gives a comparatively lower level of treatment to three other issues to which the Committee on Trade and Environment will give particular attention. The work in the Committee will include identification of any need to clarify WTO rules. The Committee will make recommendations to the Ministerial Conference on future action in these three areas, including negotiations. These three subjects are: effect of environmental measures on market access particularly for the developing countries, consideration of the relevant provisions of the TRIPS Agreement, and labelling requirements for environmental purposes.

This subject of environment follows on from Marrakesh and has been under intense consideration in the WTO since then. The major developed countries, particularly the European Union (EU), have been anxious to dilute the disciplines of Article XX of the GATT 1994 in respect of trade-restrictive measures taken in pursuance of the provisions of MEAs. The developing countries have been resisting this attempt. Now a formal negotiation will take place on this subject. Article XX of the GATT 1994 prescribes that trade restriction for environmental reasons should satisfy the test of necessity and must not be a disguised tool of trade restriction. A country taking these measures will be required to satisfy these conditions. The idea behind the proposals of the major developed countries is to have an automatic acceptance of the validity of the trade measures taken in pursuance of MEA provisions. The fear of the developing countries has been that such a move will encourage application of trade-restrictive measures in the prevailing atmosphere of protectionist pressures in the major developed countries.

It is surprising that the reduction of tariffs and non-tariff barriers on environmental goods and services has been included as a subject of negotiations under the heading of "environment". Already major negotiations have been launched in the area of tariff and non-tariff measures in the industrial products sector as discussed earlier. Also negotiations on agricultural products are going on. These negotiations will automatically cover all the goods of interest to the various participating countries. Hence the so-called "environmental goods" will also be covered by these negotiations. There is no reason, therefore, why negotiations on environmental goods should be placed under the heading of environment. It should be covered by the normal negotiations in the area of industrial goods or in the area of agriculture. In similar manner, the negotiations on environmental services should be the subject of the body handling liberalization of services.

It is important to clarify what types of goods and services are to be covered under the title of "environmental goods and services." If the idea of the proponents is to include in this class such goods which are produced in conformity with certain environmental standards, the implication is dangerous for the developing countries. It will amount to acceptance of the classification of goods based on processes and production methods (PPMs) not "related" to the goods. There is a danger of discrimination against goods, even when these goods themselves do not contain anything harmful but have been produced in a manner which is perceived as harming the environment at the place of production.

If, however, the idea is to include in this class such goods and processes which help in improving the environment, e.g., relevant machines, equipment, chemicals, etc., it is not proper to negotiate market access in respect of them separate from the general market access negotiations explained earlier. This point will be elaborated later.

Paragraph 32(i) and (ii), i.e., the subjects of the effect of environmental measures on market access and the provisions of the TRIPS Agreement, are important for the developing countries. There is a tendency in the major developed countries to curb imports on environmental grounds. There is a risk that trade-restrictive measures taken ostensibly for environmental reasons may become a new tool of protectionism in trade. Past experience has shown that usually the victims are the developing countries. It is in this context that the effect of environmental measures on market access, particularly of the developing countries, assumes importance.

The second sub-paragraph, on TRIPS and environment, has been brought in because of the experience of some developing countries that the rights of patent holders flowing out of the TRIPS Agreement have sometimes operated against the capacity of the developing countries to protect or improve the environment. Taking advantage of their monopoly position, the patent right holders sometimes dictate very severe terms for using the patented machines, chemicals and equipment. Hence a serious consideration of the subject of environment should rationally include identification of handicaps created by patent rights and the ways to solve this problem. Besides, there may be other issues regarding the linkage between TRIPS and environment, e.g., biodiversity and other matters covered by Article 27.3(b) of the TRIPS Agreement.

Paragraph 32(iii) has been brought in at the instance of some developed countries because of their need for labelling requirements on goods that pose possible environmental hazards. They argue that labelling of this nature will alert the consumer to the possible risks. The danger, though, is that the labelling requirements may cause severe strain on the exporters of the developing countries who are not well informed of the requirements and on whom the burden of providing labelling may be onerous. There is also the issue of the developing countries wanting to require labelling on environmental or safety grounds, e.g., for genetically modified foods or seeds, but facing pressures from some major developed countries to refrain from doing so.

SUGGESTED ACTION

The developing countries should ensure that the subject of tariffs and non-tariff measures on environmental goods is handled not in the negotiating body on environment, but instead by the negotiating body handling market access in industrial products (or agriculture, as the case may be). Defining what will be termed "environmental goods" should, of course, be the first step. If there is an attempt by the proponents to include in the definition the concept of "unrelated" PPMs, as explained above, it should be opposed in line with the existing stand of the developing countries. If, however, the machines, equipment, chemicals, etc. helping in the production of environmentally friendly goods are categorized as environmental goods, the major developed countries will naturally be the main exporters of such goods: hence reduction of tariff and non-tariff measures thereon will benefit them. This exercise should thus be included in the normal negotiations on tariff and non-tariff measures on industrial products, so that a proper balance of concessions can be struck. Otherwise, if it is handled in the negotiating forum for environment, it is feared that the developing countries will not be able to get reciprocal benefits in return for their reduction of the tariff and non-tariff measures on such goods.

In the negotiations on the relationship between the WTO rules and the trade obligations contained in MEAs, which is code for diluting the disciplines of Article XX of the GATT 1994, the developing countries should be careful that the disciplines not be diluted. As mentioned above, there are two essential requirements for taking trade-restrictive measures under Article XX, viz., the measures should be necessary and should not be disguised restrictions on trade. These requirements are grounded in reason and have a long history of actual implementation in the GATT/WTO. MEAs will not be in a position to weigh fully the pros and cons in respect of these two essential criteria. Hence, any suggestion that trade-restrictive action under MEAs should have automatic acceptance in the WTO without ensuring that the criteria mentioned above are satisfied, will be extremely risky. The countries whose trade will be restricted by such measures will be losing an important WTO right. And as experience has shown, the developing countries will be the main victims. Also, it is not right in principle to hand over the examination of the fulfillment of these trade criteria to some other organization.

The WTO agreements and the MEAs have been negotiated in quite separate contexts and constitute separate sets of obligations and rights. It is not correct now to mix up these rights and obligations emerging out of two completely separate sets of agreements. Moreover, an international agreement should have its own mechanism of implementation. It should not depend on another international agreement for this purpose. Thus the MEAs should themselves work out how their provisions can be effectively implemented. If the rights and obligations inscribed in the WTO are now made subservient to those in the MEAs, a wrong precedent will be set; there may be a call in future to make them subservient to the provisions of still other multilateral agreements.

There is a possibility that this line of argument may result in the major developed countries arguing that the Biodiversity Convention should not, for the same reason, be expected to modify the obligations in the

TRIPS Agreement. One solution may be to refer the conflicting obligations in the GATT 1994 and MEAs to a body like the UN to work out a reconciled position.

Apart from these basic issues, there are also some important practical problems which should be raised by the developing countries in the course of the negotiations. What should be the definition of an MEA? Multilateral agreements can be formed by even a small number of countries. Should all such agreements which cover some environmental aspects be given the status of an MEA for this purpose? If not, what should be the basis and the elements of the criteria for selecting particular agreements to be given this status? In what manner will the rights of the WTO Members that are not parties to the particular MEA be preserved? If we distinguish between WTO Members in respect of the implementation of the trade measures taken in pursuance of some MEA, will it not hit the basic MFN principle of the GATT 1994? These are only some examples; there may be several other such problems.

In respect of paragraph 32(i), the developing countries may collect information on their own experience of the past few years of their trade being restricted for environmental reasons in several major developed countries. This information will form the background for assessing the effects of environmental measures on market access of developing countries. In respect of paragraph 32(ii), they should propose qualifications to the rights of patent holders in respect of environmental products and processes.

On the labelling requirement, care should be taken that the exporters of the developing countries do not have to shoulder a heavy burden.

13 ELECTRONIC COMMERCE (PARA. 34)

BACKGROUND

This paragraph of the Ministerial Declaration has two operative points. One, the General Council has been asked to consider the most appropriate institutional arrangements for handling this subject in the Work Programme. Two, the Members have made a commitment not to impose customs duties on electronic commerce until the next Ministerial Conference.

Considering that there are already too many bodies in the WTO handling different subjects, it will not be proper to create yet another body. A preferred option may be to entrust this task to one of the existing bodies, such as the Council for Trade in Goods.

In the ongoing work in this area, which will continue, the major problem is with regard to the proposal for zero duty on electronic commerce. It is not in the interest of the developing countries to continue their commitment of zero duty in this sector. Some reasons are given below.

In the electronic commerce covered by the proposal, the exporters are generally the developed countries, whereas the developing countries are generally the importers. Except for a very few of them, the developing countries hardly have much prospect for export in this area. Hence they should not be concerned about any adverse effect arising out of other countries imposing a tax in this area. In such a situation, a pragmatic trade policy in a developing country will be more in favour of levying a tax, rather than giving up the option of taxation altogether, as is called for by the proposal on zero duty.

Even the few developing countries which have export prospects in this area will perhaps not suffer from an import tax in other countries, as their cost of production of such items is generally very low compared to that of the major exporters, i.e., the developed countries. Hence in spite of the import tax in other countries, they will generally remain competitive compared to the suppliers from the developed countries, and as such they too need not fear adverse impacts from such a tax in other countries.

There is also the important consideration of revenue. Electronic commerce is a rapidly growing activity, as is attested to by the anxiety shown by the main proponent of zero duty in this sector. Taxing this type of transaction can bring considerable resources to the government of a developing country. Committing to zero tax will foreclose all options to raise revenue from this source, resulting in huge potential loss to the government. Since developing countries generally face problems of resource shortfalls, foreclosing this option may be harmful.

Taxing this type of transaction is also fully rational and desirable from the angle of equity, particularly in the developing countries. Those engaging in these transactions are likely to be from higher income brackets, and as such it will appear to be totally iniquitous to undertake a multilateral commitment not to impose tax on them for such transactions. It is very likely that serious questions on the grounds of equity may be raised in those developing countries that make such a commitment.

And finally there is also a serious systemic question. This proposal for zero duty constitutes a discipline on a particular **mode** of transaction and not on goods or services. Agreeing to it will thus open a totally new chapter in the WTO. Its systemic implication needs careful study before there is an agreement on continuing with the commitment of zero duty.

SUGGESTIONS

There should not be a continuation of the standstill commitment on electronic commerce. Rather there should be negotiations on this request of the major developed countries, as is generally the case in the GATT/WTO process when there is a request for some concession or new commitment.

In these negotiations, the proponents, i.e., the major developed countries, should put on the table offers of reciprocal concessions. And negotiations should then take place on the request and offer.

14 TRADE, DEBT AND FINANCE (PARA. 36)

There is a broad objective in this paragraph: that there will be an examination (by a Working Group) of the relationship between trade, debt and finance. Then there are two specific tasks set out: one, to prepare some possible recommendations on steps to enhance the capacity of the multilateral trading system to contribute to a durable solution to the problem of external indebtedness of the developing countries including the least developed countries, and two, to strengthen the coherence of international trade and finance policies with a view to safeguarding the multilateral trading system from the effects of financial and monetary instability.

That there are close linkages between trade and finance has been well recognized. Also the effects of one on the other have emerged prominently in the recent experiences of some developing countries. Several experts say that trade policies and measures can be neutralized by developments in the financial sphere. Hence work on improving trade policies cannot be done in isolation from that on improving financial policies.

Moreover, there are close linkages between some parts of the WTO agreements and financial policies. For example, liberalization of financial services, examination of the elements in the area of investment, subsidization of interest on capital, change in tariffs, etc. are in several ways linked to movements of capital and exchange rate fluctuations.

The examination of this issue in the Working Group may aim at two types of results. One, there may be one set of results which will involve clarification and improvement of the WTO agreements. For example, in respect of the problem of indebtedness, the provisions in the area of market access may be very much relevant. Two, there may be a set of results which should be in the form of recommendations for consideration outside the WTO.

15 Trade and Transfer of Technology (Para. 37)

Paragraph 37 is very broad, with no specific focus for attention. But it affords the opportunity to consider how the development of technology in the developing countries can be facilitated through the use of trade instruments. This will necessarily involve consideration of the rules which can be linked to the development of technology. The agreements on TRIMs, subsidies, services and TRIPS can be easily identified for examination as to how they can be clarified and improved to encourage transfer of technology to the developing countries. Some illustrative examples are given below.

The prohibition on the domestic-content requirement by the TRIMs Agreement and Article III of the GATT 1994 can be considered as impeding technology transfer. If the developing countries are enabled to use this measure, it will encourage firms to build up domestic capacity adopting higher technology, so that the relevant domestic products are not inferior to imported products, which is often the reason why companies opt not to use domestic products. Hence it is rational to propose abolition of this restriction in the TRIMs Agreeement and Article III of the GATT 1994.

The relevant provisions in the Subsidies Agreement may be improved to enable the developing countries to provide subsidies for adoption of higher technology in production without attracting counter-actions. Such subsidies should thus be made non-actionable.

The GATS and the TRIPS Agreement may be improved to enable the developing countries to impose technology-transfer conditions on service providers and intellectual property rights holders without attracting any counter-action in the WTO.

Part II

SOME SUGGESTIONS FOR IMPROVEMENTS IN THE WTO AGREEMENTS

16 Introduction

The preparation for the World Trade Organisation (WTO) Ministerial Meeting of 1999 has started. Major developed countries have been working for a long time to place their proposals in the preparatory process. If developing countries are not ready with their concrete proposals, they will once again be only responding to the initiatives of the major developed countries, as happened in the WTO Ministerial Meetings in Singapore and Geneva. The pace of the preparatory process appears slow at present; but it is likely to gain great momentum in the new year. It is necessary for the developing countries to put up their own specific proposals as soon as possible, so that they find a place on centrestage early in the process.

The developing countries now have experience of the implementation of the WTO agreements for around four years. With that background, they are in a position to place proposals for the improvement of the agreements to bring about a degree of balance in them.

Whether the Ministerial Meeting of 1999 launches a new round of multilateral trade negotiations or whether it decides to take up only specific issues for negotiations, the developing countries should feel fully justified in putting up specific proposals for the improvement of agreements which are already in operation. In fact, the proposals for improving the existing agreements should have absolute priority over working for new agreements.

The following pages give suggestions for some specific proposals in 11 areas, viz., dispute settlement process, agriculture, services, TRIMs, TRIPS, textiles, balance-of-payments provisions, subsidies, anti-dumping, technical barriers to trade and rules of origin. More areas and proposals can be added. In each of these subjects, specific proposals have been given, preceded by a brief description of the problem and the background. For convenience, the proposals have been given in enhanced print.

17 DISPUTE SETTLEMENT UNDERSTANDING

1. REDUCTION OF COST FOR DEVELOPING COUNTRIES

The dispute settlement process is very costly. Developing countries generally weigh very carefully whether they should launch the process, even when they are convinced that their rights have been abridged or that some other country has not discharged its obligations. The cost and the resources involved in launching a case in the WTO and in following it through, may discourage many developing countries from bringing cases to the WTO dispute settlement process. This creates an imbalance in rights and obligations, as the developed countries do not have any such handicap or reservation.

The Dispute Settlement Body (DSB) or the General Council should work out specific means to reduce the cost for developing countries of effective participation in the process, either as complainant or as defendant. These means should go much beyond technical assistance.

2. RETROACTIVE COMPENSATION TO DEVELOPING COUNTRIES

If a dispute is launched by a developing country and the finding of the panel/Appellate Body is in its favour, the maximum benefit which it gets is that the other party removes the offending measure within an agreed time frame. It may take as much as nearly 30 months from the beginning of the process; and in the meantime, the trade of the developing country would have suffered damage.

In cases where a developing country is a complainant and a developed country's action is the subject of dispute, which is now found to be in violation of its obligations, the developed country should, in addition to removing the offending measure, provide adequate compensation for the period from the start of the case up to the time of complete implementation of the recommendations.

3. REIMBURSEMENT OF COST TO DEVELOPING COUNTRIES

As mentioned above, the cost of bringing a subject to the dispute settlement process is very heavy. Likewise, the cost of defence is heavy. There is a need for reimbursing the developing countries for their cost if they have been found to be right in their stand.

In cases where a developing country is either a complainant or a defendant, and the other side is a developed country, if the finding is in favour of the developing country, the developed country should pay adequate financial compensation towards the cost incurred by the developing country. The panel should make an assessment of the cost to be paid.

4. COLLECTIVE ACTION OF MEMBERS IN SOME CASES

In cases where the complaint of a country has been upheld and the defending country has not taken appropriate corrective measures within the agreed time frame, the normal practice is to authorise the complaining country to take retaliatory action against the defending country. But if the complainant is a developing country and the defendant a developed country, this final remedy is not practical, because the developing country will find it very difficult to take retaliatory action against a developed country.

There should be a provision in the Dispute Settlement Understanding for collective action by the Members of the WTO in cases where the complainant is a developing country and the defendant a developed country and the complaint of the developing country has been found to be justified.

5. REPORTS TO BE BRIEF

Recently, particularly after the formation of the WTO, the panels have developed a tendency to give very lengthy reports. Also, instead of considering the clear and direct meaning of the texts of the agreements, some panels have gone into complex legal examination. It strains the resources of the developing countries to appreciate the implication of such reports and findings. Also, when a developing country is itself a party to a dispute, it has to shoulder a heavy burden in participating in such a complex legal exercise.

The DSB or the General Council should give general guidance to panels that their reports, particularly the findings, should be brief (perhaps the maximum length can be specified), and that they should not venture into very complex legal examination, going rather by the common and direct meaning and interpretation of the texts.

6. SHORTER TIME FOR IMPLEMENTATION IN SOME CASES

In a case where a developing country is the complainant and a developed country has been asked to take corrective action as a result of the panel's/ Appellate Body's findings in favour of the developing country, the time for implementation of the recommendations should be short. The current time frame may result in a delay of up to about 30 months after the start of the process. This may be damaging to the trade interest of the developing country.

If a developing country is the complainant and a developed country is the defendant and if the complaint has been found to be justified, the developed country should be expected to take full corrective action within a maximum span of three months, if a legislative action is involved. Otherwise, it should take the corrective action within one month.

18 AGREEMENT ON AGRICULTURE

1. DOMESTIC SUPPORT AND EXPORT SUBSIDY IN DEVELOPED COUNTRIES

The developed countries undertook commitments to reduce their domestic support, budgetary outlay for export subsidy and the quantity of export covered by export subsidy by 20, 36 and 21 per cent respectively over the period of 1995-2000. Thus the bulk of their domestic support and export subsidy will continue to be applicable even beyond 2000. The farmers of developed countries have enjoyed protection and support for a long time in the past. They are much more endowed with resources and enjoy a much more favourable environment of production and export, compared to farmers in developing countries. The domestic support and export subsidy provided by the governments in developed countries are further enhancing the unfair advantage which the farmers in developed countries have over those in developing countries.

Developed countries should totally eliminate their domestic support and export subsidy immediately, the latest by 2005. They should accordingly provide schedules for their domestic support and export subsidy applicable from 2001 onwards until 2005, by the end of which the levels should be zero.

2. TARIFF IN DEVELOPED COUNTRIES

In the process of tariffication, developed countries have recorded very high tariffs in their schedules. Their farmers have benefited from protection for a very long time, earlier through direct import control measures and lately by prohibitive tariffs. In fact, the developed countries undertook a commitment to reduce the tariffs only by 36 per cent during the period 1995-2000. Continuation of such a high level of protection of agriculture in developed countries is patently unfair.

Developed countries should reduce their tariffs significantly during the five years beyond 2000. There should be a rational ceiling on their tariff peaks.

3. DOMESTIC SUPPORT AND EXPORT SUBSIDY IN DEVELOPING COUNTRIES

The developing countries which did not apply domestic support and export subsidy measures earlier, have naturally not recorded them in their schedules; and thereby they have been debarred from applying these measures in future beyond the *de minimis* levels. This is highly iniquitous. As their farmers generally are in a disadvantaged position, compared to those in developed countries, it is only fair to lift this restriction.

In the context of Article 3 of the agreement, there should be an understanding that developing countries will not be subjected to this restriction. Similarly, the developing countries that have given their schedules of reduction of domestic support and export subsidy should be allowed flexibility to enhance the levels of these measures or to lessen the pace of reduction of the levels. If an understanding on Article 3 is not considered sufficient for this purpose, there should be a specific additional provision in Article 3 for this purpose.

4. LIFTING OF RESTRICTIONS FOR ENCOURAGING FOOD PRODUCTION

It will be dangerous for developing countries to depend on imported food, as their foreign exchange position is often not comfortable, and the provision of food for the population is essential. Hence, what is needed is that developing countries should be encouraged to produce food for their domestic population. The current disciplines on import control and domestic support may hamper their efforts in this direction.

The food products in developing countries should be excluded from the disciplines of import control and domestic support. It should be done, either through a clarification of Articles 3 and 4 of the agreement, or, if need be, through an additional provision in the agreement to this effect.

5. REMOVAL OF INIQUITY IN ARTICLE 13

The "due restraint" provision in Article 13 is unbalanced and iniquitous. Subsidies covered by Annex 2, which are generally prevalent in developed countries, have been made immune from countermeasures and countervailing duty action; whereas subsidies which are generally prevalent in developing countries, e.g., investment subsidy and input subsidy, covered by Article 6, do not have this dispensation. This discrimination is patently unfair and it should be removed.

The subsidies of developing countries, covered by Article 6, should be made immune from countermeasures and countervailing duty action. Article 13 should be modified accordingly.

6. SUPPORT TO HOUSEHOLD FARMERS AND SMALL FARMERS

In a large number of developing countries, many farmers take to agriculture not as a commercial venture, but as a family activity passed down over generations. This is in the nature of subsistence cultivation at the household level. Also, many developing countries have a large number of small farmers, whose farming activities will not be able to stand up to a large scale of international competition. They need protection, otherwise there will be large-scale unemployment and spread of poverty in these countries.

Developing countries should have flexibility regarding import restraint and domestic subsidy for the protection of and support to household subsistence farming and small-scale farming. There should be requisite clarification in Articles 3 and 4 for this purpose. If considered necessary, there should be an additional provision for this purpose.

7. REMOVAL OF UNPREDICTABILITY ABOUT DOMESTIC SUBSIDY

A country can modulate the choice of product and the rate of subsidy to match the ceiling of domestic support in a particular year. This causes uncertainty in the minds of exporters in other countries, who do not know which products will be covered by the reduction and to what extent. Hence, exporters in other countries may have difficulty in planning their exports. There is a need to remove this uncertainty.

Countries should plan out the products and the levels of support a few years in advance and it should be notified. There should be an understanding in this regard.

8. RELIEF TO NET FOOD-IMPORTING COUNTRIES

The current provision regarding relief to the net food-importing developing countries does not contain specific and concrete action for the relief. In fact, hardly anything has been done in this regard. There is a need for some specific action to provide relief to these countries. There should be more operational and effective provisions for this purpose.

One way could be to have a fund for this purpose, to which contributions should be made by the developed countries which are major exporters of agricultural products. Specific criteria for contributions to the fund should be worked out and made enforceable in the agreement.

19 GENERAL AGREEMENT ON TRADE IN SERVICES

1. IMBALANCE IN THE BENEFITS

This agreement, which is for the liberalisation of import of services, directly benefits, at least in the short term, mainly the countries which are endowed with a developed level of services. The downstream effects on production and other economic activities can be beneficial also for the importing countries; but the direct positive effects on export earnings are in the exporting countries. And in this area, developed countries are the main exporters. Hence, the distribution of direct gains as between developed and developing countries through the liberalisation of services is very much in favour of developed countries. It is necessary to remove this imbalance.

The agreement should have provisions for specific commitments by developed countries to import services from developing countries whenever the latter are in a position to supply such services. There should also be commitments by developed countries for specific measures to enhance the supply capacity of developing countries. These commitments should not be in the nature of a "best endeavour" clause; they should be enforceable commitments. For example, some of the commitments could be in respect of the following:

(i)   exemption of developing countries from the application of the limitations, conditions and qualifications mentioned by developed countries in their schedules for Articles XVI and XVII of GATS;

(ii)   enhanced degree of access and entry facilities for the service providers of developing countries in the developed countries (at present, in several cases there is less facility of access to the developed countries for the service providers of developing countries);

(iii)   positive structural adjustment in the services sectors in developed countries so as to encourage the use of particular services in respect of which the developing countries have supply capacity;

(iv)   reservation of a predetermined portion of specified services used by the governments in developed countries for supplies from developing countries; and

(v)   provision of incentives to private and public entities for import of services from developing countries.

2. IMBALANCE BETWEEN CAPITAL AND LABOUR

The movement of capital has been specifically included in the obligations, but the same treatment has not been given to the movement of labour. Article XI says that restrictions must not be applied on international transfers and payments for current transactions relating to specific sectoral commitments. Further, it says that there must not be any restriction on capital transactions which is inconsistent with the specific sectoral commitments. Then, according to Article XVI, where cross-border movement of capital is an essential part of the movement of service in which a commitment has been made by a country, that country is committed to allowing such movement. Also, when the commitment in respect of the supply of service is through commercial presence, a country is committed to allowing related transfers of capital. There are no similar provisions about the movement of labour.

There should be a provision in the agreement that there must not be any restriction on the movement of labour which is inconsistent with the specific sectoral commitments and where cross-border movement of labour is an essential part of the supply of service for which commitments have been made in Article XVI.

3. SUBSIDIES AND NATIONAL TREATMENT

In the area of goods, subsidy to domestic industry is exempted from the obligation of national treatment in accordance with Article III.8(b) of GATT 1994. In GATS, there is no such provision, with the result that subsidies provided to domestic services will also have to be provided to services of foreign origin, except if specific conditionalities have been included in the schedule under Article XVII of GATS. It is necessary to have a specific provision for exempting subsidies from the obligation of national treatment as in the case of goods.

There should be a provision either in Article XVII or in Article XV of GATS, laying down that subsidies to domestic services or service providers will be exempted from the obligation of national treatment.

4. RECOGNITION OF EDUCATION AND EXPERIENCE

The recognition of education and experience, licences, certificates, etc can make a major difference to the market access of services. Article VII of GATS provides for recognition by a Member of the education, experience, etc obtained in a country. There is a likelihood of discrimination against the developing countries in this matter. There is a need for safeguard against unjustified denial of recognition to them. The process of dispute settlement will not be relevant or useful for this purpose.

GATS should have a provision for the Council for Trade in Services to attend to the problems faced by Members, particularly the developing countries, and to resolve them so that complete fairness in the process of recognition is ensured.

5. IMPLEMENTATION OF SPECIAL PROVISIONS FOR DEVELOPING COUNTRIES

Articles IV and XIX.2 of GATS have special provisions for the developing countries. These provisions have, however, not been put into practice. Instead of being given special consideration, developing countries have, in fact, been targeted for extraction of commitments in important sectors like financial services. There is a need for serious and sincere implementation of the special provisions for developing countries as envisaged in the agreement.

GATS should have a specific provision for monitoring the implementation of these commitments. For example, the Council for Trade in Services may have periodic consultations with developed countries to examine how they are implementing these provisions. Besides, a developing country may be encouraged to bring before the Council, cases of non-implementation, which should be considered in the format of consultation with the particular developed country.

20 AGREEMENT ON TRIMS

1. DOMESTIC CONTENT REQUIREMENT

The Agreement on Trade-Related Investment Measures (TRIMs) specifically prohibits application of the domestic content requirement. It has resulted in a major handicap for developing countries. The domestic content requirement is useful and often necessary for: (i) encouraging domestic economic activities in raw material and intermediate input sectors, (ii) upgradation of input production, (iii) prevention of wastage of foreign exchange in the import of raw materials and intermediate inputs, (iv) ensuring linkages of foreign direct investment with domestic economic activities, (v) encouraging indigenisation in the case of foreign direct investment, (vi) acting in several other ways as an important instrument in the development process, etc.

Earlier, when there was more flexibility in respect of balance-of-payments (BOP) measures, the use of domestic products could be ensured through direct restraints on import of the corresponding products. Now, with the constraints on this flexibility, the need for domestic content requirement is further enhanced. It is important for developing countries to have the flexibility to apply domestic content requirement.

Developing countries should be exempted from the disciplines on the application of domestic content requirement. There is a need for an enabling provision in Article 2 or 4 of the agreement to this effect.

2. LIMITATION ON IMPORT OF INPUTS

At present there is a restriction on putting limitation to the import of inputs. It cannot be limited to a certain percentage of the exports of the entity. Thus the restriction inhibits a developing country from having balancing of foreign exchange. In view of the precarious foreign exchange position of the developing countries, it is necessary that this flexibility is available to them.

Developing countries should be exempted from the discipline of not limiting the import of inputs. There is a need for an enabling provision in Article 2 or 4 to this effect.

21 Agreement on TRIPS[1]

Two provisions of the Agreement on Trade-Related Aspects of Intellectual Property Rights (TRIPS) will come up for review in 1999. These are Article 27.3(b) relating to plants and animals, and Article 64 relating to dispute settlement. Developing countries need to put up their proposals during these reviews. Besides, it will also be useful to put up suggestions for the improvement of some other parts of the agreement. Some suggestions are given below.

ARTICLE 27.3(b)

Article 27.3(b) of the Agreement on TRIPS has three main components, viz.:

I.   A country **may** exclude from patentability: (i) plants, (ii) animals and (iii) essentially biological processes for the production of plants and animals.

II. A country **must** allow patents for: (i)micro-organisms, and (ii) non-biological and microbiological processes of production of plants and animals.

III. A country **must** provide for the protection of plant varieties, either through patents or through an **effective *sui generis* system**.

1. The occurrence of "may" in item I above, creates an impression that there is a possibility for a country to allow the patenting of plants and animals. Hence there is a need for clarity to the effect that patenting of naturally occurring plants and animals, including their parts, must not be allowed. It is important as the big firms and research persons working in this area in the developed countries, have been exploiting the natural bio-resources of developing countries through the patenting process. This need for clarity applies to the gene sequence as well, which is very much a part of the particular plant or animal.

There should be a formal clarification that naturally occurring plants, animals, the parts of plants and animals, including the gene sequence, and essentially biological processes for the production of plants, animals and their parts, must not be granted patents.

2. The terms "micro-organisms" and "non-biological and microbiological processes" have not been specifically defined. Hence there is scope for interpretation and clarification in their application.

There should be a clarification that the term "micro-organisms" used here does not refer to naturally occurring micro-organisms, e.g., naturally occurring bacteria, fungi, algae, protozoa or viruses.

3. There have been instances in the recent past when firms in developed countries have obtained patents for the use of naturally occurring plants in some developing countries with some slight modifications. Such uses of these plants have been in practice in these countries for a long time; and therefore such patenting is totally wrong. There is a need for clarification of the criterion of novelty in such cases.

There should be a decision that patents must not be granted for a subject matter which was available to the public by means of use, written description or in any other manner in any country, prior to the date of filing of the application for patents. This principle should also

apply to subject matters which have been in use by local and indigenous communities.

4.   It is necessary to prevent the patenting of plant materials obtained from collections held in international germplasm banks and other deposit institutions where such materials are publicly available.

There should be a decision that no patents should be granted for such materials. Also, if patents have been granted, these should be cancelled, if it comes to the notice of the authorities that the subject matter of the patent fits the description given above.

5.   When the subject matter of a patent application is derived from the plant material of a country, the consent of the country must be obtained before granting the patent. Besides, the Convention on Biological Diversity (CBD) has laid down certain principles in its Article 15, which should be fully respected while considering an application for patents on materials derived from the bio-resources of a country.

There should be a decision to incorporate a provision that patents must not be granted in such cases without the prior consent of the country of origin. Also, patents inconsistent with Article 15 of the CBD must not be granted.

6.   If the subject matter of a patent is derived from the bio-resources of a country, it should be obligatory on the patent holder to share the economic benefits of the patent with the country of origin and also with the indigenous communities that have nurtured the bio-resources for a long time.

There should be a decision that a country must impose such a condition on the patent holder who must faithfully implement it.

7. In the interest of enhancing knowledge and supporting development, there may be a need for the patent-granting country to allow use of the subject matter for scientific experiments and breeding.

There should be a decision to provide for the right to a country to allow free use of the subject matter for scientific experimental use and breeding.

8. In the term "effective *sui generis* system" mentioned in item III above, there are two elements. First, what would be a *sui generis* system, and second, how will its effectiveness be determined. Those who are signatories to UPOV (the International Convention for the Protection of New Varieties of Plants) 1991 or are likely to be signatories in the near future, will argue that the minimum standards of an effective *sui generis* system would be those which are in UPOV 1991. Their line of argument may be that UPOV 1991 got evolved because the earlier agreement, viz., UPOV 1978, was not found to be adequate. This point needs to be strongly opposed. It will be quite proper to argue that a country is free to choose its own *sui generis* system, and also that a country has to decide by itself what is an effective system. The test of effectiveness should not be the subject of multilateral examination.

There should be an understanding that a country has the right to formulate and adopt a *sui generis* system for the protection of plant varieties.

DISPUTE SETTLEMENT

9. The general dispute settlement mechanism of the WTO lays down three preconditions for taking recourse to the dispute settlement process. A country should have suffered nullification or impairment of benefits, or the objectives of a particular agreement should have been impeded, by:

(i) the failure of another country to carry out its obligations, or (ii) the application by another country of any measure, whether or not it conflicts with the provisions of an agreement, or (iii) the existence of any other situation. In the case of the Agreement on TRIPS, only the element in (i) above is applicable at present. The review in 1999 will examine the need for the applicability of the other two elements. In this agreement, it is more likely that the developing countries will be defendants in disputes, rather than complainants. Hence it is desirable not to expand the scope of the dispute settlement process.

The current provision should continue, and the elements of (ii) and (iii) should not be brought into the dispute settlement process.

PROCEDURE FOR COMPULSORY LICENSING

10. The current procedure in Article 31 for the use of patents without authorisation is highly restrictive. In particular, it limits the authorisation to the supply to domestic markets and it provides for termination of the authorisation if the circumstances which led to it cease to exist. Both these provisions would severely discourage any entrepreneur from proposing to use the patent. The first provision mentioned above restricts the use and the second one creates economic and commercial uncertainty.

These two restrictions on compulsory licensing should be removed.

COMPULSORY LICENSING FOR ESSENTIAL DRUGS

11. Certain drugs are essential and any restriction on their production should be removed so as to make them available in ample quantities at reasonable prices. There is a need for relaxation of the exclusive rights of the patent holders in respect of these drugs. In order not to make this relaxation indiscriminate, it could be limited to the drugs listed by the World Health Organisation (WHO) as essential. Such relaxation will be fully in the spirit of the principles contained in Article 8.

There should be a provision authorising countries to use automatic compulsory licensing for these drugs in the interest of their supply at reasonable prices in the country. Thus the procedure of Article 31 need not be followed in this case.

UNILATERAL ACTION

12.   Article 301 of the US Trade Act provides for retaliation against a country for the protection of intellectual property rights (IPRs), even if the country has complied with the obligations of the Agreement on TRIPS.

There should be a decision explicitly and clearly prohibiting the use of unilateral measures such as the one mentioned above.

THE REFERENCE DATE FOR PRIORITY

13.   For the purpose of priority, some countries use the criterion of first to invent, rather than first to file. The determination of first to invent is often problematic. In the use of this criterion in different countries, difficulties may be encountered.

There should be a clarification that the criterion of first to file will be applicable.

22 AGREEMENT ON TEXTILES AND CLOTHING

1. STRUCTURAL ADJUSTMENT IN DEVELOPED COUNTRIES

The agreement envisaged a comparatively smooth transition of the special regime in textiles to the normal WTO regime as applied to other goods sectors. If the progressive liberalisation process had been sincerely implemented with that objective in view, the developed countries would not have covered only a very small portion of restrained items in the liberalisation process during the four years of implementation. Past experience shows that developed countries are very much swayed by their industry in this sector to ignore their commitments in the international trade regime and go slow on any normalisation process. There is a reasonable fear that this trend may be repeated in future too. Hence there is a need for special efforts to facilitate the transition of the textile regime in the developed countries from now till 2004. Developed countries have to take specific measures so that their industry is not faced with the problem of sudden adjustment.

The agreement should have a provision for positive structural adjustment efforts by governments in the developed countries. They should prepare positive structural adjustment programmes and send them to the WTO, where timely implementation of the programmes should be kept under review.

2. RAPID LIBERALISATION IN DEVELOPED COUNTRIES

The pace of liberalisation in the developed countries in respect of the products covered by import restraints has been very slow. It has two major implications. First, the spirit of progressive liberalisation has not been followed. Second, the process of liberalisation, which was already very much backloaded, has become much more so, with the result that the industry in the developed countries will be suddenly required to adjust to rapid liberalisation later, as mentioned above. Hence it is necessary that the developed countries introduce a much faster pace of liberalisation immediately.

The developed countries should cover 33 per cent of their import of restrained products in the liberalisation process within one year, i.e., by the end of 1999.

3. ABSTAINING FROM ANTI-DUMPING ACTION

In view of the specific practices of import controls in this sector in the developed countries, the industry gets unduly disturbed when the imports increase or when it apprehends dangers of competition from developing countries. The experience of the past has shown that they take recourse to the easy method of sponsoring anti-dumping action against the imports from developing countries. In the spirit of liberalisation and as a token of good faith in restoring the textiles sector to the normal WTO rules, the developed countries should discourage such tendencies in their industry. There is a need for a "peace clause" in this sector in respect of anti-dumping action.

There should be a provision in the agreement for a moratorium in the developed countries on anti-dumping action in this sector against the imports from developing countries until the entire textile sector in these countries is brought within the normal WTO rules.

4. RULES OF ORIGIN

Recently some major developed countries have introduced rules of origin which need to be changed, as they do not correspond to the reality of the situation. The developing exporting countries suffer, because imports get assigned to them even though the products were actually exported by some other countries. Hence the rules of origin now introduced have gravely restrained the market access of textiles from the developing countries. The situation needs to be corrected.

The rules of origin should be immediately modified so that the countries of origin are correctly assigned based on the rational criteria of the manufacture of the product.

23 UNDERSTANDING ON BOP PROVISIONS

1. EXISTENCE OF BOP PROBLEM

In examining whether a country is facing a BOP problem, at present the foreign exchange reserves and net foreign exchange inflow are taken into account. The composition and the nature of the foreign exchange reserves and inflow are generally not considered. This creates major problems. The foreign exchange reserves of a country may have some unstable elements which cannot be depended upon for commitment of foreign exchange expenditure. For example, short-term deposits or portfolio investments in foreign exchange may swell the reserves, and yet may not be quite useful in meeting the commitment of a country in repayments in foreign exchange, and to that extent, may not really contribute to the improvement of the BOP situation. Hence there is a need to have an understanding on the factors which should be taken into account while considering the existence of a BOP problem in a developing country.

The composition of the reserves and inflow of foreign exchange should be an important factor in determining whether a BOP problem exists in a country. The elements of the reserves and inflow which are of an uncertain, unstable and short-term nature, should be excluded in examining the adequacy of foreign exchange.

2. NEED FOR FOREIGN EXCHANGE

Normally at present, the need for foreign exchange is determined on the basis of the expenditure in the past few years. This consideration is inadequate and faulty. Sometimes developing countries try to move on a fast track of development and they may need foreign exchange in excess of the historical trend of expenditure for this purpose. Hence there is a need for improvement in the method of assessing the need for foreign exchange.

The need for foreign exchange should be assessed on the basis of the development programme of the country concerned, i.e., it should be guided by future programmes, rather than the historical trend of expenditure.

3. FLEXIBILITY ON THE MEASURES TO BE ADOPTED

The Understanding on BOP Provisions has put a constraint on the developing countries in respect of the measures they can take to ease their BOP problems. It says that non-price measures, e.g., direct import control etc, should be taken only after it is demonstrated that price measures, e.g., raising of customs duty, are not effective. The developing countries with BOP problems need the measures to have a quick and assured effect on their imports. And it is well known that direct import control measures are much more effective and quick in this regard than price measures like raising of tariffs. Hence the restriction put on the developing countries by the Understanding on the type of measures to be taken should be completely removed.

A developing country facing a BOP problem should be quite free to choose the type of measures for easing and solving the problem.

24 Agreement on Subsidies and Countervailing Measures

1. SOME SUBSIDIES TO BE MADE NON-ACTIONABLE

There is a grave imbalance in the agreement in respect of declaring some subsidies non-actionable. The subsidies which are normally used in developed countries, viz., those for research and development, regional development and adaptation to environmental standards, have been declared non-actionable. But the subsidies which are normally used by developing countries for development, diversification and upgradation, are actionable in the sense that counter-action can be taken against them under certain conditions. This imbalance has to be removed immediately.

The subsidies used by developing countries for development, diversification and upgradation of their industry and agriculture should be made non-actionable. Thus action should not be taken against them either through the dispute settlement route or through the countervailing duty route.

2. PROTECTION OF IMPORT SUBSTITUTION SUBSIDY

Article 27.3 of the agreement allows developing countries to grant subsidy for the use of domestic products in preference to the imported product (defined in Article 3.1(b) of the agreement). Now some doubts are being raised about the application of this provision in view of the restriction in the Agreement on TRIMs on the domestic content requirement. There is a need to clarify unambiguously that the provision of Article 27.3 is applicable.

There should be clarification in Article 27.3 that the provision is applicable notwithstanding the provisions of any other agreement.

3. EXPORT COMPETITIVENESS

Article 27.5 of the agreement requires a developing country to phase out its export subsidy when it reaches the stage of export competitiveness (defined in Article 27.6). Thus there is an automatic exclusion from this benefit on reaching the stage of export competitiveness. There is no clarity as to what will happen if a developing country loses export competitiveness.

There should be a provision in Article 27 for automatic removal of this disability of a developing country, once it loses export competitiveness.

4. ELIGIBILITY FOR INCLUSION IN ANNEX VII

Countries have been included in Annex VII (thereby enjoying special dispensation in respect of subsidies) on the criterion of their per capita Gross National Product (GNP) being less than US$1,000 per annum. Once the level of per capita GNP rises above this level, a country is likely to be excluded from this list. It is proper to wait for some time before a country is excluded, in order to see whether or not the higher level of GNP per capita is stable. Further, there is no provision at present for automatic inclusion of a developing country in this annex if its per capita GNP falls to this critical level.

There should be a provision in Annex VII to the effect that a developing country will be excluded from the annex only if its GNP per capita remains above the critical level mentioned in the annex for a continu-

ous period of two years. Also, there should be a provision in the annex that a developing country will be automatically included in this annex if its GNP per capita falls to this critical level.

25 AGREEMENT ON ANTI-DUMPING

1. RESTORING ANTI-DUMPING TO THE NORMAL DISPUTE SETTLEMENT PROCESS

Article 17.6 of the Agreement on Anti-dumping has practically excluded the anti-dumping cases from the normal dispute settlement process by restricting the role of the dispute settlement panels. The panels, in such cases, can only determine whether the anti-dumping authorities have established the facts properly and whether their evaluation of the facts has been unbiased and objective. Further, if there are two or more permissible interpretations of any provision, the interpretation of the domestic authorities will be held valid if they have followed one of these interpretations, even though the panel may itself disagree with the interpretation. In disputes on all other subjects, the panels have a much broader role, particularly in determining whether a country has violated its obligation under the particular agreement. This basic role has been denied to the panels in the anti-dumping cases. As the developing countries are generally the harassed victims in such cases, the constraint on the role of the panels has grossly reduced their capacity to get relief. There is a need to restore the anti-dumping cases to the normal dispute settlement process.

Article 17.6 should be removed.

2. PROTECTION AGAINST REPEATED HARASSMENT

Often developing countries have been the victims of repeated anti-dumping investigations in respect of the same or similar products. Industry in developed countries has the tendency to use the provision of anti-dumping investigations for protectionist purposes. There is a need to discourage, and in fact stop, this tendency. One way could be to have punitive provisions for frivolous complaints.

There should be a provision in the agreement that countries should provide for punishment of an industry which has been complaining repeatedly, if the complaints have not been found suitable for imposition of anti-dumping duty. Also there should be a provision of payment of financial compensation to the developing country, if the complaint has been found to be frivolous or non-substantiated.

3. *DE MINIMIS* LEVELS FOR DEVELOPING COUNTRIES

The developing countries have been harassed with anti-dumping investigations and duties for a long time now. The defence against these investigations is proving to be very costly to them. There is a need to provide them with some protection. One important way could be to have *de minimis* levels in their cases below which they will not be subjected to anti-dumping investigation.

There should be a special *de minimis* provision that a developing country will not be subjected to anti-dumping investigation or duty, if the margin of dumping is less than 15 per cent, or if the volume of the alleged dumped import is less than 5 per cent of the total import of the product in the importing country.

4. PRESUMPTION OF DUMPING IN THE CASE OF DEVELOPED COUNTRIES

As developing countries are now liberalising their imports, the incidence of dumping into these countries may increase. And they may find it very costly and difficult to take anti-dumping action against the imports from developed countries. There is a need to provide protection to developing countries against dumping from the developed countries, otherwise the momentum of their import liberalisation may be checked. The problem of the developing countries in this regard can be somewhat relieved if, in the event of imports from developed countries to developing countries, there is a provision of presumption of dumping when certain conditions are fulfilled. We have, as an example, the presumption of the existence of serious prejudice caused by the subsidies of developed countries in the event of certain conditions having been met (Article 6.1 of the Agreement on Subsidies).

There should be a provision in the agreement for presumption of dumping under certain conditions in the case of imports from developed countries into developing countries. The elements of these conditions could be worked out by the Council for Trade in Goods.

26 AGREEMENT ON TECHNICAL BARRIERS TO TRADE

The agreement gives primacy to international standards. If international standards exist for a product or are imminent, a Member is generally obliged to adopt them, except if it can be demonstrated that these standards are ineffective or inappropriate. Further, international standards have the benefit of the presumption that they do not create an unnecessary obstacle to international trade. These standards are in the process of being formulated.

The standards play an important role in the market access of goods. The implications of setting a particular standard for a product go much beyond the technical quality of the product; the standards define whether the product of a country will be permitted to be imported in different markets. The developing countries have to be on the watch in respect of the formulation of international standards for two reasons. First, it has to be ensured that the standard is not being set at too high a level for meeting the objectives of safety and other requirements. This caution is needed as the firms in the developed countries may be inclined to have very high standards which they can easily incorporate in their products, but which may be very difficult for the firms of developing countries to adopt, because of their financial and technological handicaps. Second, as the international standard-setting body may not be very familiar with the conditions in the developing countries, their special attributes in respect of their products, production process and materials may be ignored. It is therefore necessary for the developing countries to participate in the working out of international standards.

But developing countries do not have adequate resources. They do not have suitable personnel in adequate numbers or financial resources for this purpose. Hence effective ways have to be worked out so that their interests are fully taken into account. This process should go much beyond merely providing technical assistance to them.

The Council for Trade in Goods should deliberate seriously on this matter and adopt some specific means for safeguarding the interests of the developing countries in the formulation of international standards. It should be appropriately incorporated in the Agreement on Technical Barriers to Trade.

27 AGREEMENT ON RULES OF ORIGIN

With the process of globalisation of production and products passing through several countries in various stages of production, the rules of origin have assumed great importance. Whenever the access of goods will depend on the country of origin, the rules of origin will influence the market access significantly. The developing countries have recently been experimenting with various methods of ownership of their production firms and establishing international linkages of production. The rules of origin are very important in this context as well.

Currently, exercises are ongoing for finalising the rules of origin. The Agreement on Rules of Origin has given guidelines for this purpose. The developing countries, however, are not able to participate effectively in this process because of their paucity of resources. They do not have adequate numbers of trained personnel, nor do they have adequate financial resources for participating in the technical meetings and discussions on this subject. If their interests are not fully taken into account, they may ultimately lose out on the market access of such goods where the rules of origin are critical in obtaining permission to import.

The Council for Trade in Goods should deliberate on this issue seriously and work out ways of facilitating the participation of the developing countries in the process of formulation of the rules of origin. It should go much beyond providing technical assistance. The objective should be to have a balanced set of rules keeping the interests of the developing countries fully in view. The ways worked out by the Council should be incorporated in the agreement.

ANNEX

Doha Ministerial Declaration
Adopted on 14 November 2001

1.   The multilateral trading system embodied in the World Trade Organization has contributed significantly to economic growth, development and employment throughout the past fifty years. We are determined, particularly in the light of the global economic slowdown, to maintain the process of reform and liberalization of trade policies, thus ensuring that the system plays its full part in promoting recovery, growth and development. We therefore strongly reaffirm the principles and objectives set out in the Marrakesh Agreement Establishing the World Trade Organization, and pledge to reject the use of protectionism.

2.   International trade can play a major role in the promotion of economic development and the alleviation of poverty. We recognize the need for all our peoples to benefit from the increased opportunities and welfare gains that the multilateral trading system generates. The majority of WTO Members are developing countries. We seek to place their needs and interests at the heart of the Work Programme adopted in this Declaration. Recalling the Preamble to the Marrakesh Agreement, we shall continue to make positive efforts designed to ensure that developing countries, and especially the least-developed among them, secure a share in the growth of world trade commensurate with the needs of their economic development. In this context, enhanced market access, balanced rules, and well targeted, sustainably financed technical assistance and capacity-building programmes have important roles to play.

3.   We recognize the particular vulnerability of the least-developed countries and the special structural difficulties they face in the global economy. We are committed to addressing the marginalization of least-developed countries in international trade and to improving their effective participation in the multilateral trading system. We recall the commitments made by Ministers at our meetings in Marrakesh, Singapore and Geneva, and by the international community at the Third UN Conference on Least-Developed Countries in Brussels, to help least-developed countries secure beneficial and meaningful integration into the multilateral trading system and the global economy. We are determined that the WTO will play its part in building effectively on these commitments under the Work Programme we are establishing.

4.   We stress our commitment to the WTO as the unique forum for global trade rule-making and liberalization, while also recognizing that regional trade agreements

can play an important role in promoting the liberalization and expansion of trade and in fostering development.

5.   We are aware that the challenges Members face in a rapidly changing international environment cannot be addressed through measures taken in the trade field alone. We shall continue to work with the Bretton Woods institutions for greater coherence in global economic policy-making.

6.   We strongly reaffirm our commitment to the objective of sustainable development, as stated in the Preamble to the Marrakesh Agreement. We are convinced that the aims of upholding and safeguarding an open and non-discriminatory multilateral trading system, and acting for the protection of the environment and the promotion of sustainable development can and must be mutually supportive. We take note of the efforts by Members to conduct national environmental assessments of trade policies on a voluntary basis. We recognize that under WTO rules no country should be prevented from taking measures for the protection of human, animal or plant life or health, or of the environment at the levels it considers appropriate, subject to the requirement that they are not applied in a manner which would constitute a means of arbitrary or unjustifiable discrimination between countries where the same conditions prevail, or a disguised restriction on international trade, and are otherwise in accordance with the provisions of the WTO Agreements. We welcome the WTO's continued cooperation with UNEP and other inter-governmental environmental organizations. We encourage efforts to promote cooperation between the WTO and relevant international environmental and developmental organizations, especially in the lead-up to the World Summit on Sustainable Development to be held in Johannesburg, South Africa, in September 2002.

7.   We reaffirm the right of Members under the General Agreement on Trade in Services to regulate, and to introduce new regulations on, the supply of services.

8.   We reaffirm our declaration made at the Singapore Ministerial Conference regarding internationally recognized core labour standards. We take note of work under way in the International Labour Organization (ILO) on the social dimension of globalization.

9.   We note with particular satisfaction that this Conference has completed the WTO accession procedures for China and Chinese Taipei. We also welcome the accession as new Members, since our last Session, of Albania, Croatia, Georgia, Jordan, Lithuania, Moldova and Oman, and note the extensive market-access commitments already made by these countries on accession. These accessions will greatly strengthen the multilateral trading system, as will those of the 28 countries now negotiating their accession. We therefore attach great importance to concluding accession proceedings as quickly as possible. In particular, we are committed to accelerating the accession of least-developed countries.

10. Recognizing the challenges posed by an expanding WTO membership, we confirm our collective responsibility to ensure internal transparency and the effective participation of all Members. While emphasizing the intergovernmental character of the organization, we are committed to making the WTO's operations more

transparent, including through more effective and prompt dissemination of information, and to improve dialogue with the public. We shall therefore at the national and multilateral levels continue to promote a better public understanding of the WTO and to communicate the benefits of a liberal, rules-based multilateral trading system.

11. In view of these considerations, we hereby agree to undertake the broad and balanced Work Programme set out below. This incorporates both an expanded negotiating agenda and other important decisions and activities necessary to address the challenges facing the multilateral trading system.

WORK PROGRAMME

Implementation-related issues and concerns

12. We attach the utmost importance to the implementation-related issues and concerns raised by Members and are determined to find appropriate solutions to them. In this connection, and having regard to the General Council Decisions of 3 May and 15 December 2000, we further adopt the Decision on Implementation-Related Issues and Concerns in document WT/MIN(01)/17 to address a number of implementation problems faced by Members. We agree that negotiations on outstanding implementation issues shall be an integral part of the Work Programme we are establishing, and that agreements reached at an early stage in these negotiations shall be treated in accordance with the provisions of paragraph 47 below. In this regard, we shall proceed as follows: (a) where we provide a specific negotiating mandate in this Declaration, the relevant implementation issues shall be addressed under that mandate; (b) the other outstanding implementation issues shall be addressed as a matter of priority by the relevant WTO bodies, which shall report to the Trade Negotiations Committee, established under paragraph 46 below, by the end of 2002 for appropriate action.

Agriculture

13. We recognize the work already undertaken in the negotiations initiated in early 2000 under Article 20 of the Agreement on Agriculture, including the large number of negotiating proposals submitted on behalf of a total of 121 Members. We recall the long-term objective referred to in the Agreement to establish a fair and market-oriented trading system through a programme of fundamental reform encompassing strengthened rules and specific commitments on support and protection in order to correct and prevent restrictions and distortions in world agricultural markets. We reconfirm our commitment to this programme. Building on the work carried out to date and without prejudging the outcome of the negotiations we commit ourselves to comprehensive negotiations aimed at: substantial improvements in market access; reductions of, with a view to phasing out, all forms of export subsidies; and substantial reductions in trade-distorting domestic support. We agree that special and differential treatment for developing countries shall be an integral part of all elements of the negotiations and shall be embodied in the Schedules of concessions and commitments and as appropriate in the rules and

disciplines to be negotiated, so as to be operationally effective and to enable developing countries to effectively take account of their development needs, including food security and rural development. We take note of the non-trade concerns reflected in the negotiating proposals submitted by Members and confirm that non-trade concerns will be taken into account in the negotiations as provided for in the Agreement on Agriculture.

14. Modalities for the further commitments, including provisions for special and differential treatment, shall be established no later than 31 March 2003. Participants shall submit their comprehensive draft Schedules based on these modalities no later than the date of the Fifth Session of the Ministerial Conference. The negotiations, including with respect to rules and disciplines and related legal texts, shall be concluded as part and at the date of conclusion of the negotiating agenda as a whole.

Services

15. The negotiations on trade in services shall be conducted with a view to promoting the economic growth of all trading partners and the development of developing and least-developed countries. We recognize the work already undertaken in the negotiations, initiated in January 2000 under Article XIX of the General Agreement on Trade in Services, and the large number of proposals submitted by Members on a wide range of sectors and several horizontal issues, as well as on movement of natural persons. We reaffirm the Guidelines and Procedures for the Negotiations adopted by the Council for Trade in Services on 28 March 2001 as the basis for continuing the negotiations, with a view to achieving the objectives of the General Agreement on Trade in Services, as stipulated in the Preamble, Article IV and Article XIX of that Agreement. Participants shall submit initial requests for specific commitments by 30 June 2002 and initial offers by 31 March 2003.

Market access for non-agricultural products

16. We agree to negotiations which shall aim, by modalities to be agreed, to reduce or as appropriate eliminate tariffs, including the reduction or elimination of tariff peaks, high tariffs, and tariff escalation, as well as non-tariff barriers, in particular on products of export interest to developing countries. Product coverage shall be comprehensive and without *a priori* exclusions. The negotiations shall take fully into account the special needs and interests of developing and least-developed country participants, including through less than full reciprocity in reduction commitments, in accordance with the relevant provisions of Article XXVIII *bis* of GATT 1994 and the provisions cited in paragraph 50 below. To this end, the modalities to be agreed will include appropriate studies and capacity-building measures to assist least-developed countries to participate effectively in the negotiations.

Trade-related aspects of intellectual property rights

17. We stress the importance we attach to implementation and interpretation of the Agreement on Trade-Related Aspects of Intellectual Property Rights (TRIPS Agreement) in a manner supportive of public health, by promoting both access to existing

medicines and research and development into new medicines and, in this connection, are adopting a separate Declaration.

18. With a view to completing the work started in the Council for Trade-Related Aspects of Intellectual Property Rights (Council for TRIPS) on the implementation of Article 23.4, we agree to negotiate the establishment of a multilateral system of notification and registration of geographical indications for wines and spirits by the Fifth Session of the Ministerial Conference. We note that issues related to the extension of the protection of geographical indications provided for in Article 23 to products other than wines and spirits will be addressed in the Council for TRIPS pursuant to paragraph 12 of this Declaration.

19. We instruct the Council for TRIPS, in pursuing its work programme including under the review of Article 27.3(b), the review of the implementation of the TRIPS Agreement under Article 71.1 and the work foreseen pursuant to paragraph 12 of this Declaration, to examine, *inter alia*, the relationship between the TRIPS Agreement and the Convention on Biological Diversity, the protection of traditional knowledge and folklore, and other relevant new developments raised by Members pursuant to Article 71.1. In undertaking this work, the TRIPS Council shall be guided by the objectives and principles set out in Articles 7 and 8 of the TRIPS Agreement and shall take fully into account the development dimension.

Relationship between trade and investment

20. Recognizing the case for a multilateral framework to secure transparent, stable and predictable conditions for long-term cross-border investment, particularly foreign direct investment, that will contribute to the expansion of trade, and the need for enhanced technical assistance and capacity-building in this area as referred to in paragraph 21, we agree that negotiations will take place after the Fifth Session of the Ministerial Conference on the basis of a decision to be taken, by explicit consensus, at that Session on modalities of negotiations.

21. We recognize the needs of developing and least-developed countries for enhanced support for technical assistance and capacity building in this area, including policy analysis and development so that they may better evaluate the implications of closer multilateral cooperation for their development policies and objectives, and human and institutional development. To this end, we shall work in cooperation with other relevant intergovernmental organizations, including UNCTAD, and through appropriate regional and bilateral channels, to provide strengthened and adequately resourced assistance to respond to these needs.

22. In the period until the Fifth Session, further work in the Working Group on the Relationship Between Trade and Investment will focus on the clarification of: scope and definition; transparency; non-discrimination; modalities for pre-establishment commitments based on a GATS-type, positive list approach; development provisions; exceptions and balance-of-payments safeguards; consultation and the settlement of disputes between Members. Any framework should reflect in a balanced manner the interests of home and host countries, and take due account of

the development policies and objectives of host governments as well as their right to regulate in the public interest. The special development, trade and financial needs of developing and least-developed countries should be taken into account as an integral part of any framework, which should enable Members to undertake obligations and commitments commensurate with their individual needs and circumstances. Due regard should be paid to other relevant WTO provisions. Account should be taken, as appropriate, of existing bilateral and regional arrangements on investment.

Interaction between trade and competition policy

23. Recognizing the case for a multilateral framework to enhance the contribution of competition policy to international trade and development, and the need for enhanced technical assistance and capacity-building in this area as referred to in paragraph 24, we agree that negotiations will take place after the Fifth Session of the Ministerial Conference on the basis of a decision to be taken, by explicit consensus, at that Session on modalities of negotiations.

24. We recognize the needs of developing and least-developed countries for enhanced support for technical assistance and capacity building in this area, including policy analysis and development so that they may better evaluate the implications of closer multilateral cooperation for their development policies and objectives, and human and institutional development. To this end, we shall work in cooperation with other relevant intergovernmental organizations, including UNCTAD, and through appropriate regional and bilateral channels, to provide strengthened and adequately resourced assistance to respond to these needs.

25. In the period until the Fifth Session, further work in the Working Group on the Interaction between Trade and Competition Policy will focus on the clarification of: core principles, including transparency, non-discrimination and procedural fairness, and provisions on hardcore cartels; modalities for voluntary cooperation; and support for progressive reinforcement of competition institutions in developing countries through capacity building. Full account shall be taken of the needs of developing and least-developed country participants and appropriate flexibility provided to address them.

Transparency in government procurement

26. Recognizing the case for a multilateral agreement on transparency in government procurement and the need for enhanced technical assistance and capacity building in this area, we agree that negotiations will take place after the Fifth Session of the Ministerial Conference on the basis of a decision to be taken, by explicit consensus, at that Session on modalities of negotiations. These negotiations will build on the progress made in the Working Group on Transparency in Government Procurement by that time and take into account participants' development priorities, especially those of least-developed country participants. Negotiations shall be limited to the transparency aspects and therefore will not restrict the scope for countries to give preferences to domestic supplies and suppliers. We commit

ourselves to ensuring adequate technical assistance and support for capacity building both during the negotiations and after their conclusion.

Trade facilitation

27. Recognizing the case for further expediting the movement, release and clearance of goods, including goods in transit, and the need for enhanced technical assistance and capacity building in this area, we agree that negotiations will take place after the Fifth Session of the Ministerial Conference on the basis of a decision to be taken, by explicit consensus, at that Session on modalities of negotiations. In the period until the Fifth Session, the Council for Trade in Goods shall review and as appropriate, clarify and improve relevant aspects of Articles V, VIII and X of the GATT 1994 and identify the trade facilitation needs and priorities of Members, in particular developing and least-developed countries. We commit ourselves to ensuring adequate technical assistance and support for capacity building in this area.

WTO rules

28. In the light of experience and of the increasing application of these instruments by Members, we agree to negotiations aimed at clarifying and improving disciplines under the Agreements on Implementation of Article VI of the GATT 1994 and on Subsidies and Countervailing Measures, while preserving the basic concepts, principles and effectiveness of these Agreements and their instruments and objectives, and taking into account the needs of developing and least-developed participants. In the initial phase of the negotiations, participants will indicate the provisions, including disciplines on trade distorting practices, that they seek to clarify and improve in the subsequent phase. In the context of these negotiations, participants shall also aim to clarify and improve WTO disciplines on fisheries subsidies, taking into account the importance of this sector to developing countries. We note that fisheries subsidies are also referred to in paragraph 31.

29. We also agree to negotiations aimed at clarifying and improving disciplines and procedures under the existing WTO provisions applying to regional trade agreements. The negotiations shall take into account the developmental aspects of regional trade agreements.

Dispute Settlement Understanding

30. We agree to negotiations on improvements and clarifications of the Dispute Settlement Understanding. The negotiations should be based on the work done thus far as well as any additional proposals by Members, and aim to agree on improvements and clarifications not later than May 2003, at which time we will take steps to ensure that the results enter into force as soon as possible thereafter.

Trade and environment

31. With a view to enhancing the mutual supportiveness of trade and environment, we agree to negotiations, without prejudging their outcome, on:

(i)   the relationship between existing WTO rules and specific trade obligations set out in multilateral environmental agreements (MEAs). The negotiations shall be limited in scope to the applicability of such existing WTO rules as among parties to the MEA in question. The negotiations shall not prejudice the WTO rights of any Member that is not a party to the MEA in question;

(ii) procedures for regular information exchange between MEA Secretariats and the relevant WTO committees, and the criteria for the granting of observer status;

(iii) the reduction or, as appropriate, elimination of tariff and non-tariff barriers to environmental goods and services.

We note that fisheries subsidies form part of the negotiations provided for in paragraph 28.

32. We instruct the Committee on Trade and Environment, in pursuing work on all items on its agenda within its current terms of reference, to give particular attention to:

(i)   the effect of environmental measures on market access, especially in relation to developing countries, in particular the least-developed among them, and those situations in which the elimination or reduction of trade restrictions and distortions would benefit trade, the environment and development;

(ii) the relevant provisions of the Agreement on Trade-Related Aspects of Intellectual Property Rights; and

(iii) labelling requirements for environmental purposes.

Work on these issues should include the identification of any need to clarify relevant WTO rules. The Committee shall report to the Fifth Session of the Ministerial Conference, and make recommendations, where appropriate, with respect to future action, including the desirability of negotiations. The outcome of this work as well as the negotiations carried out under paragraph 31(i) and (ii) shall be compatible with the open and non-discriminatory nature of the multilateral trading system, shall not add to or diminish the rights and obligations of Members under existing WTO agreements, in particular the Agreement on the Application of Sanitary and Phytosanitary Measures, nor alter the balance of these rights and obligations, and will take into account the needs of developing and least-developed countries.

33. We recognize the importance of technical assistance and capacity building in the field of trade and environment to developing countries, in particular the least-developed among them. We also encourage that expertise and experience be shared with Members wishing to perform environmental reviews at the national level. A report shall be prepared on these activities for the Fifth Session.

Electronic commerce

34. We take note of the work which has been done in the General Council and other relevant bodies since the Ministerial Declaration of 20 May 1998 and agree to continue the Work Programme on Electronic Commerce. The work to date demonstrates that electronic commerce creates new challenges and opportunities for trade

for Members at all stages of development, and we recognize the importance of creating and maintaining an environment which is favourable to the future development of electronic commerce. We instruct the General Council to consider the most appropriate institutional arrangements for handling the Work Programme, and to report on further progress to the Fifth Session of the Ministerial Conference. We declare that Members will maintain their current practice of not imposing customs duties on electronic transmissions until the Fifth Session.

Small economies

35. We agree to a work programme, under the auspices of the General Council, to examine issues relating to the trade of small economies. The objective of this work is to frame responses to the trade-related issues identified for the fuller integration of small, vulnerable economies into the multilateral trading system, and not to create a sub-category of WTO Members. The General Council shall review the work programme and make recommendations for action to the Fifth Session of the Ministerial Conference.

Trade, debt and finance

36. We agree to an examination, in a Working Group under the auspices of the General Council, of the relationship between trade, debt and finance, and of any possible recommendations on steps that might be taken within the mandate and competence of the WTO to enhance the capacity of the multilateral trading system to contribute to a durable solution to the problem of external indebtedness of developing and least-developed countries, and to strengthen the coherence of international trade and financial policies, with a view to safeguarding the multilateral trading system from the effects of financial and monetary instability. The General Council shall report to the Fifth Session of the Ministerial Conference on progress in the examination.

Trade and transfer of technology

37. We agree to an examination, in a Working Group under the auspices of the General Council, of the relationship between trade and transfer of technology, and of any possible recommendations on steps that might be taken within the mandate of the WTO to increase flows of technology to developing countries. The General Council shall report to the Fifth Session of the Ministerial Conference on progress in the examination.

Technical cooperation and capacity building

38. We confirm that technical cooperation and capacity building are core elements of the development dimension of the multilateral trading system, and we welcome and endorse the New Strategy for WTO Technical Cooperation for Capacity Building, Growth and Integration. We instruct the Secretariat, in coordination with other relevant agencies, to support domestic efforts for mainstreaming trade into national plans for economic development and strategies for poverty reduction. The delivery of WTO technical assistance shall be designed to assist developing and

least-developed countries and low-income countries in transition to adjust to WTO rules and disciplines, implement obligations and exercise the rights of membership, including drawing on the benefits of an open, rules-based multilateral trading system. Priority shall also be accorded to small, vulnerable, and transition economies, as well as to Members and Observers without representation in Geneva. We reaffirm our support for the valuable work of the International Trade Centre, which should be enhanced.

39. We underscore the urgent necessity for the effective coordinated delivery of technical assistance with bilateral donors, in the OECD Development Assistance Committee and relevant international and regional intergovernmental institutions, within a coherent policy framework and timetable. In the coordinated delivery of technical assistance, we instruct the Director-General to consult with the relevant agencies, bilateral donors and beneficiaries, to identify ways of enhancing and rationalizing the Integrated Framework for Trade-Related Technical Assistance to Least-Developed Countries and the Joint Integrated Technical Assistance Programme (JITAP).

40. We agree that there is a need for technical assistance to benefit from secure and predictable funding. We therefore instruct the Committee on Budget, Finance and Administration to develop a plan for adoption by the General Council in December 2001 that will ensure long-term funding for WTO technical assistance at an overall level no lower than that of the current year and commensurate with the activities outlined above.

41. We have established firm commitments on technical cooperation and capacity building in various paragraphs in this Ministerial Declaration. We reaffirm these specific commitments contained in paragraphs 16, 21, 24, 26, 27, 33, 38-40, 42 and 43, and also reaffirm the understanding in paragraph 2 on the important role of sustainably financed technical assistance and capacity-building programmes. We instruct the Director-General to report to the Fifth Session of the Ministerial Conference, with an interim report to the General Council in December 2002 on the implementation and adequacy of these commitments in the identified paragraphs.

Least-developed countries

42. We acknowledge the seriousness of the concerns expressed by the least-developed countries (LDCs) in the Zanzibar Declaration adopted by their Ministers in July 2001. We recognize that the integration of the LDCs into the multilateral trading system requires meaningful market access, support for the diversification of their production and export base, and trade-related technical assistance and capacity building. We agree that the meaningful integration of LDCs into the trading system and the global economy will involve efforts by all WTO Members. We commit ourselves to the objective of duty-free, quota-free market access for products originating from LDCs. In this regard, we welcome the significant market access improvements by WTO Members in advance of the Third UN Conference on LDCs (LDC-III), in Brussels, May 2001. We further commit ourselves to consider additional measures for progressive improvements in market access for LDCs.

Accession of LDCs remains a priority for the Membership. We agree to work to facilitate and accelerate negotiations with acceding LDCs. We instruct the Secretariat to reflect the priority we attach to LDCs' accessions in the annual plans for technical assistance. We reaffirm the commitments we undertook at LDC-III, and agree that the WTO should take into account, in designing its work programme for LDCs, the trade-related elements of the Brussels Declaration and Programme of Action, consistent with the WTO's mandate, adopted at LDC-III. We instruct the Sub-Committee for Least-Developed Countries to design such a work programme and to report on the agreed work programme to the General Council at its first meeting in 2002.

43. We endorse the Integrated Framework for Trade-Related Technical Assistance to Least-Developed Countries (IF) as a viable model for LDCs' trade development. We urge development partners to significantly increase contributions to the IF Trust Fund and WTO extra-budgetary trust funds in favour of LDCs. We urge the core agencies, in coordination with development partners, to explore the enhancement of the IF with a view to addressing the supply-side constraints of LDCs and the extension of the model to all LDCs, following the review of the IF and the appraisal of the ongoing Pilot Scheme in selected LDCs. We request the Director-General, following coordination with heads of the other agencies, to provide an interim report to the General Council in December 2002 and a full report to the Fifth Session of the Ministerial Conference on all issues affecting LDCs.

Special and differential treatment

44. We reaffirm that provisions for special and differential treatment are an integral part of the WTO Agreements. We note the concerns expressed regarding their operation in addressing specific constraints faced by developing countries, particularly least-developed countries. In that connection, we also note that some Members have proposed a Framework Agreement on Special and Differential Treatment (WT/GC/W/442). We therefore agree that all special and differential treatment provisions shall be reviewed with a view to strengthening them and making them more precise, effective and operational. In this connection, we endorse the work programme on special and differential treatment set out in the Decision on Implementation-Related Issues and Concerns.

ORGANIZATION AND MANAGEMENT OF THE WORK PROGRAMME

45. The negotiations to be pursued under the terms of this Declaration shall be concluded not later than 1 January 2005. The Fifth Session of the Ministerial Conference will take stock of progress in the negotiations, provide any necessary political guidance, and take decisions as necessary. When the results of the negotiations in all areas have been established, a Special Session of the Ministerial Conference will be held to take decisions regarding the adoption and implementation of those results.

46. The overall conduct of the negotiations shall be supervised by a Trade Negotiations Committee under the authority of the General Council. The Trade Negotia-

tions Committee shall hold its first meeting not later than 31 January 2002. It shall establish appropriate negotiating mechanisms as required and supervise the progress of the negotiations.

47. With the exception of the improvements and clarifications of the Dispute Settlement Understanding, the conduct, conclusion and entry into force of the outcome of the negotiations shall be treated as parts of a single undertaking. However, agreements reached at an early stage may be implemented on a provisional or a definitive basis. Early agreements shall be taken into account in assessing the overall balance of the negotiations.

48. Negotiations shall be open to:

(i) all Members of the WTO; and
(ii) States and separate customs territories currently in the process of accession and those that inform Members, at a regular meeting of the General Council, of their intention to negotiate the terms of their membership and for whom an accession working party is established.

Decisions on the outcomes of the negotiations shall be taken only by WTO Members.

49. The negotiations shall be conducted in a transparent manner among participants, in order to facilitate the effective participation of all. They shall be conducted with a view to ensuring benefits to all participants and to achieving an overall balance in the outcome of the negotiations.

50. The negotiations and the other aspects of the Work Programme shall take fully into account the principle of special and differential treatment for developing and least-developed countries embodied in: Part IV of the GATT 1994; the Decision of 28 November 1979 on Differential and More Favourable Treatment, Reciprocity and Fuller Participation of Developing Countries; the Uruguay Round Decision on Measures in Favour of Least-Developed Countries; and all other relevant WTO provisions.

51. The Committee on Trade and Development and the Committee on Trade and Environment shall, within their respective mandates, each act as a forum to identify and debate developmental and environmental aspects of the negotiations, in order to help achieve the objective of having sustainable development appropriately reflected.

52. Those elements of the Work Programme which do not involve negotiations are also accorded a high priority. They shall be pursued under the overall supervision of the General Council, which shall report on progress to the Fifth Session of the Ministerial Conference.